MEDICAL INTUITION

MEDICAL INTUITION

How to Combine Inner Resources
with Modern Medicine

*a journey of
self-discovery
and healing*

RUTH BERGER

SAMUEL WEISER, INC.
York Beach, Maine

First published in 1995 by
SAMUEL WEISER, INC.
P.O. Box 612
York Beach, ME 03910-0612

Library of Congress Cataloging-in-Publication-Data

Berger, Ruth
          Medical intuition : how to combine inner
    resources with modern medicine / Ruth Berger.
          p.   cm.
    1. Healing. 2. Intuition. I. Title.
    RZ999.B47   1995
    610 — dc20   95-19107
    ISBN 0-87728-851-8   CIP

CCP
Cover art "Touching Hands," copyright © 1995 Dale O'Dell.
Used by permission.
Typeset in 11 point Book Antiqua

PRINTED IN THE UNITED STATES OF AMERICA

00 99 98 97 96 95
10 9 8 7 6 5 4 3 2 1

The paper used in this publication meets the minimum requirements of the
American National Standard for Permanence of Paper of the Printed Library
Materials Z39.48-1984

ABOUT THIS BOOK....

People will "see" their illnesses as growth opportunities.

People will not fear their illnesses.

People will be educated about their illnesses.

People will select doctors who communicate with them.

People will keep their power.

*People will study how past lives influence their
present condition.*

People will be able to utilize any form of alternative healing.

People will never again say, "It's incurable."

*Everyone will know how to do
Medical Intuition.*

Table of Contents

Advance Praise ix

Acknowledgments xi

Chapter 1   You Can Do It. 1

Chapter 2   Trusting Yourself 3

Chapter 3   Doubting Less. 9

Chapter 4   Faith. 14

Chapter 5   Listening to Your Body 19

Chapter 6   Identifying Fear 24

Chapter 7   Why You Get Sick 27

Chapter 8   Understanding Your Past 31

Chapter 9   Trusting Your Creativity 36

Chapter 10   Believing in Your Future 40

Chapter 11   Releasing the Pain of the Past 43

Chapter 12   Understanding Your Dreams 48

Chapter 13   Seeing Clearly. 54

Chapter 14   Transforming Fears 57

Chapter 15   Letting Go of Pain 62

Chapter 16   Balancing Logic and Creativity 66

Chapter 17   Finding Energy Blocks 71

Chapter 18   Transforming Energy Blocks 75

Chapter 19   Knowing When to Say Yes 79

Chapter 20   Don't Judge Yourself 84

Chapter 21   You Can Be Wrong 87

Chapter 22   Loving Your Fears 91

Chapter 23   Loneliness Ends 94

Chapter 24   Darkness Becomes Light 97

Chapter 25   The Right Person 102

Chapter 26   Use Your Fears as Tools 108

Chapter 27   Creating Love and Order 114

Chapter 28   Learning About Your Illness 119

Chapter 29   Finding the Right Healer 123

Chapter 30   The Root of Your Disease 126

Chapter 31   Making Choices 132

Chapter 32   Knowing Your Rights 135

Chapter 33   Healing the Mind 138

About the Author 144

Advance Praise

IT IS AN HONOR to prepare the way for Ruth Berger. I believe you will enjoy, be inspired, and treasure *Medical Intuition*.

I have known Ruth Berger in her many facets as teacher, wife, mother, writer, speaker, friend, psychic, and listener. Ruth lives, teaches, and writes with enormous enthusiasm and with the same commitment and passion that is so richly stored in this book. Much love and understanding of humanity is what Ruth offers you, the reader.

You should always remember that we do not have to learn some new discipline to arrive at our own center, because in reality we never really depart from it. Each person can evoke his or her potentialities for growth. Each is, or can be, his or her own architect. Ruth, in her own way, laid the groundwork for an awakening in all of us.

—OSCAR G. RASMUSSEN, PH.D.

Although this book has many techniques for developing one's own intuitive abilities, it seems to me that its greatest value is in teaching self-healing. I suggest if you are interested in personal development, you use Ruth Berger's book to set your own house in order. Once that happens, then you may be ready to move into helping others.

—C. NORMAN SHEALY, M.D., PH.D.

I see many people in this day and age who are seeking to develop their psychic ability because they know that there is so much there that needs awakening and yet, they have no place to go that is really reliable for help in this development. I also see these people getting into situations of developing their psychic ability and getting totally confused because there are no ideas and no direction being manifested by the people doing the teaching.

I particularly appreciate Ruth Berger's awareness, centering of the work, and consciousness on the divine plan.

I found Ruth's book most interesting and helpful. I think the information is clear and well-presented. The steps identified are understandable and could be followed with clarity by a person seriously interested in developing Medical Intuition.

—GLADYS T. MCGAREY, M.D.

Acknowledgments

To my soulmate Dan—who traveled my journey with me. Thank you.

To my daughter Penny—who has been my intuitive teacher, guard, and student throughout her life. Thank you.

To my daughter Karri—who at times is my mother, my medical researcher, and my friend. Thank you.

To my son Craig—who has taught me patience and unconditional love. Thank you.

To my granddaughters Christie, Shannon, and Dana for their intuitive inputs. Thank you.

To Mary Laney for her encouragement and journalistic input. Thank you.

I am indebted to the following individuals for their healing abilities: Dr. Paul V. Johnson and Robert Ericcson of the Spiritual Advisory Council; Dr. Rudolph Ballentine of the Himalayan Institute;

Dr. William and John McGarey and all the healers of the A.R.E. Medical Clinic; Dr. Andrew Pasminski, Adella Zumas, Harriet Braun, Lythia Pavlon, Lee Toman, Morton Cohen, and Rev. LeRoy E. Zemke.

Thank you!

• • •

INSPIRATIONAL WORDS and thoughts from famous people appear at the beginning of each chapter. They are taken from the following sources: John Locke (page 19), Nicolas Malebranche (page 40), T.S. Eliot (page 54), Seneca (page 57), Matthew Arnold (page 75), Albert Einstein (page 79), Oliver Wendall Holmes (page 84), Aristotle (page 123), George Moore (page 132), Benjamin Disraeli (page 135), Kahlil Gibran (page 138), and Samuel Johnson (page 142) from *International Thesaurus of Quotations*, Rhoda Thomas Tripp, ed. (New York: HarperCollins, 1970); Bernard M. Baruch (page 3), Franklin Delano Roosevelt (page 24), Publilius Syrus (page 27), Ralph Waldo Emerson (pages 36 and 71), Nathaniel Hawthorne (page 43), Mahatma Gandhi (page 87), an Arabian Proverb (page 91), Louis L. Mann (page 94), Tryon Edwards (page 102), Alfred North Whitehead (page 114), Lord Byron (page 119) from *Instant Quotation Dictionary*, Donald O. Bolander, B.S., M.A., ed. (Mundelein, IL: Career Publishers,

1969); William Hazlitt (page 62), Friedrich W. Nietzsche (page 108), and Sebastien Roch Nicolas Chamfort (page 126) from *The Great Thoughts*, George Seldes, ed. (New York: Ballantine, 1985); Thomas Fuller (page 9) and Mother Teresa (page 48) from *The Harper Book of Quotations*, Robert I. Fitzhenry, ed. (New York: HarperCollins, 1993); John F. Kennedy (page 14) from *Speaker's Lifetime Library*, Leonard and Thelma Spinrad (Englewood Cliffs, NJ: Prentice Hall, 1961).

1

You Can Do It

You've got a disease. The doctors are wonderful but they offer no hope. They don't know what else to do for you and neither do you. You become a guinea pig, hoping some magical treatment will be discovered in time. What do you do next?

Listening, learning, and loving your body is the real cure.

Get depressed—get angry—become convinced there are no solutions, no options, nothing. A hungry beast called fear takes over. Its pointed, sharp teeth begin eating away all hope of you ever getting well.

You think of committing suicide, killing the doctors, or laying back and imagining a better life.

You go to a psychiatrist who listens, writes things down, and says, "Get your mind off your illness. Do some exercises, listen to positive thinking tapes, watch happy television shows, and do activities that make you feel good."

You return home inspired, wanting to do it all. You call up a friend and talk. Soon you're tired and sick again. The fear monster returns.

What's missing from this picture? Why is it you're not getting better? Maybe it's because your head has been chopped open with an ax and all anyone is giving you to treat it is a Band-Aid?

Your body is screaming in pain and no one is helping. All you're doing is waiting for someone else to do something. Stop waiting and start listening to what your body is trying to tell you. You've tried everything else.

Listening, learning, and loving your body is the real cure. Medical Intuition opens your mind to other healing alternatives.

✳

Medical Intuition is something you can do.

2

Trusting Yourself

MEDICAL INTUITION SETS YOU on a journey of self-discovery. You read everything you can about your illness and find it troubling. There are only a few procedures and you've tried them all. Nothing has worked. If you're going to get well, you'll have to find a new method. But where do you find that information?

A friend calls. "There is going to be a Medical Intuition seminar about alternative healing choices. Want to go?"

When one door closes, another opens.

You say, "I'll be there."

The first speaker talked about how he'd overcome advanced emphysema.

"First I got a hay fever allergy, then it developed into asthma, and finally into advanced emphysema. Six doctors said I had a life threatening disease and that nothing could be done.

"There are no such things as incurables, there are only things for which man has not found a cure."

—BERNARD M. BARUCH, APRIL 1954

"I'd never smoked. One medical specialist said my lungs were so pure, they were easy to contaminate. I'd have been better off if I'd smoked a little.

"My allergies worked counter-productively with medications. Migraine headaches would often result within an hour after ingesting a new medicine. Depression would set in because the medication would force me to go to bed in the middle of my work day.

"My life was a nightmare. Everywhere we went in those days, people smoked. If I got one whiff of a cigarette, I'd go immediately into an emphysema attack. Paramedics would be called to assist me. Often I'd have to go to the hospital emergency room for added help.

"Curious what it's like to be taken to a hospital in an ambulance?

"It's terrifying! Driving through red lights with cars trying to beat the ambulance through the intersection was more frightening than not being able to breathe.

"I was terrified to go out in public and too depressed to stay home. The doctors said my disease would only get worse.

"I wanted to get well but every door was closed to me until I went to an intuitive consultant with advanced intuitive abilities, who gave me a health reading.

"The consultant suggested finding a holistic doctor, one who believes that meditation, nutrition, stress reduction techniques, natural foods, teas, and vitamins could enhance my wellness.

"I went to three health food stores to ask who the staff would recommend. They all said the same physician's name. I made an appointment with the doctor and began Medical Intuition training.

"First I had to stop eating all the foods I liked and eat rice three times a day. The doctor wanted me to stabilize my body. I'd been eating sweets instead of healthy foods for most of my meals.

"I was taught yoga to master my body and learned how to breathe like a new baby.

"My doctor told me to go for a walk every day regardless of the weather. That winter was one of Chicago's coldest.

"I walked every day and found the cold air refreshing. This from a person who thinks the day isn't warm unless the temperature is 70 or above.

"A daily discipline of proper eating, yoga, and breathing exercises required a lot of concentration and will power. Weekly emphysema attacks kept me focused on getting well.

"After a year-and-a-half went by without any visible signs of healing, I became despondent and returned to my old way of living: eating junk foods, lots of sugar, and no meditation.

"I got so sick I thought I would die right then. When I recovered a week later, I remembered what it used to be like: the coughing spasms, the exhaustion, and the terrible fear that consumed my every waking thought. I wasn't going to fall into that trap again.

"Another year went by. My wife and I took a trip out west from Chicago. I'd taken my oxygen tank along just in case. I was still having emphysema attacks, but hoped the vacation would relax me and help me feel better.

"It must have been farmer's chemicals in the air that triggered an emphysema attack. I couldn't breathe and my oxygen tank only had 9 minutes left in it. Not enough to get me to the next town, some 25 miles away. Monster fears set in.

"We swiftly closed the car windows and set the air conditioner to the highest setting.

"My wife drove the car like a madwoman. In my fear, I looked to her for support. Her face was drained of all color. Her eyes were bulging out and her knuckles were white from holding the wheel so tight. She, too, was bitten by the monster fear. I looked at her and in that instant realized she might have a heart attack and die before me.

"I had to save her. I vowed I would not be the reason for her death. My will to save her overcame my fear of not being able to get my next breath. I forced my mind to recall every healing technique I'd been taught.

"'Take short breaths,' I remembered my trainer's words. 'Think only of how to breathe easily and effortlessly. Relax your shoulders. Do a gentle head roll. Don't think about anything except how to breathe. Stay focused.'

"I closed my eyes and willed my mind to master my anxiety. I needed all my energy to force my body to relax and stop gasping for air. I did head rolls and prayed a lot.

"I remember one woman saying an emphysema attack was like someone holding your nose and mouth closed, and asking you to stay calm.

"I needed oxygen. I didn't want to suck in air and start hyperventilating. Like a paramedic pumping air into someone's chest, I concentrated on breathing correctly.

"'Inhale through your mouth and visualize the oxygen flowing into your chest and down into your stomach,' my trainer had drilled into my head. 'You will learn to breathe correctly and be able to control an emphysema attack. Trust yourself.'

"Soon my body began to relax and breathe normally. Euphoria set in as I realized I'd been able to control my body and overcome my fear.

"Twenty-five minutes later, I was out of danger and so was my wife. We began to laugh from relief.

I'd never known such bliss. I discovered how I could control my mind and body.

"I'd like to say that was the end of my emphysema attacks, but it wasn't. I needed three more years of correct diet, meditation, exercise, and discipline before I was able to throw away my three oxygen tanks.

"Today, twenty years later, I can swim forty laps, bike fifteen miles, hike up a mountain, and live a normal life.

"Medical Intuition taught me to trust me."

All afternoon you listened to this speaker talk about how he overcame his advanced emphysema.

You wondered, "Could I control my pain?"

You were tired but your mind wanted to hear more.

✳

Medical Intuition teaches self trust.

3

Doubting Less

SPEAKER #2 SAID, "When you're little, you don't analyze and worry about what others think. You just cry for what you want. Later you learn to stifle your feelings and separate from what your body needs.

"Parents and teachers want their students to behave. You try to be what you think they want.

"Later you want to be accepted by the other teenagers, so you dress and act just like them.

"Wanting to be accepted by everyone except yourself takes you further and further from who you really are.

> *"Trust thyself only, and another shall not betray thee."*
>
> —THOMAS FULLER, M.D.

"Eventually, you became fearful of making the wrong choices.

"Medical Intuition is learning to trust your instincts more and doubting less.

"Sickness is more than a physical symptom. Sickness is a separation from who you really are.

"A backache might represent a friend who dumps too much on you, and you feel *you have to* solve his problems.

"A headache might occur because you don't want to do something, but do it anyway because you feel you *should.*

"Legs, feet may become sluggish because you *don't trust* yourself enough to take a risk and get out of your rut.

"Chest pains are often due to a *lack* of self love.

"Stomachaches occur when you *stop* liking yourself.

"Low back pains may result from too many *doubts* about yourself and others.

"Every pain is your body's way of trying to get your attention. If you don't listen to the early warnings, your body will become sickly.

"When you trust your instincts, you find the right medical people to treat you.

"Imagine having chest pains. You could get caught up in self-diagnosis. You don't think logically.

"You may be suffering from eating too many fatty foods, or taking on the emotions of the people you love, or maybe you're having a heart attack!

"You need more information before making the correct choice.

"Your body will tell you what it needs, if you learn to listen with all your senses.

"Most people stop their intuitive flow by interrupting their psychic flow. They jump to conclusions and overanalyze. No wonder their hunches are wrong so much of the time!

"Step 1. Trust your feelings.

"A hunch is a sudden insight about someone or something. It may not be based in logic.

First comes the hunch;

Then comes the crunch;

And out goes the punch.

"Example: You're having a pleasant dinner with a friend. When she begins talking about her new boyfriend, you suddenly become fearful. Your head starts hurting. The more she talks about him, the worse your head aches.

"Your head is trying to tell you something. Listen. Don't interrupt with mind games:

"I'm probably coming down with a cold.

"I'm tired.

"I've got to get out of here.

"Step 2. Stop running. Start listening. Trust your intuition. Activate your senses by thinking like a detective. Ask yourself:

"What triggered the pain?

"Answer: Listening to your friend talk about her new boyfriend.

"Why did I get upset?

"Answer: My friend has a history of meeting abusive men.

"Why?

"Answer: She doesn't know this guy is like all the rest. My intuition tells me this guy could really hurt her bad. I don't want to say the wrong thing and cut her off. What should I do?

"a) Share my feelings and take the risk of losing my friend?

"b) Give some excuse to leave.

"c) Get more intuitive information.

"Police warn people to be sensitive to danger. Stop, if you suddenly feel fearful while walking to your car.

"Step 3. Listen to which answer lessens the pain.

"The third answer lessens your headache. You start asking questions of your friend. 'Do you feel safe when you're with this guy?'

"Tears suddenly well up in your friend's eyes. 'Sometimes,' she says. 'But I don't have any reason not to trust him.'

"'Trust your feelings,' you say. The pain in your head is gone.

"Paying attention to your intuition may save someone's life.

"The secret to validating your intuition is not stopping to analyze any of it until you've got it all.

"The more you doubt, the more you interrupt the correct intuitive message.

"Fear is the number one obstacle in self-trust. Stop getting in the way of your intuition. Trusting your instincts will help you make better choices and your body will stop sending you sick messages."

The afternoon ended with you getting hungry and hoping you wouldn't have to eat junk food.

✳

Medical Intuition means doubting less – trusting more.

4

Faith

Faith healing—come one, come all. You read the notice and think, "The conference was making sense until now. This reads like a side show." You want to leave, but your curiosity keeps you from bolting out the door.

> *"Let both sides seek to invoke the wonders of science instead of its terrors. Together let us explore the stars, conquer the deserts, eradicate disease, tap the ocean depths. . .*
> — John F. Kennedy, 1961

You observe the people entering the faith healing area. They are smiling and nodding hello to one another. They seem normal enough. You decide to attend, but will be cautious.

In the front of the room, six empty chairs face the audience. Someone is playing the piano with a melody you've never heard before. You like the music. It calms you.

"Close your eyes to shut off distractions," says the speaker. "Let go of all your business and personal concerns as you do this exercise.

"Notice how smoothly or bumpy you inhale and exhale. Concentrate on inhaling smoothly. Focus on this for a few moments.

"Now imagine yourself relaxing on a bed of soft grass, looking up at the blue sky. Watch the birds flying back and forth and notice the white clouds in the distance.

"Notice a white funnel of light behind the clouds coming toward you."

You can't take your eyes away. You watch the light getting brighter as it gets closer to you. The light feels warm and soothing as it touches your body. It feels so good, you don't want it to stop.

You realize your body isn't hurting and you're not in a hurry to analyze why. "That's a switch," you think with a big grin.

The speaker says, "Enjoy the music and just let your body relax. This is your time to be with God."

You feel serene, less apprehensive, but still don't want to become a victim. You open one eye and see people standing behind the empty chairs waiting. A few people in the audience are walking to the chairs. They sit down and close their eyes.

The people behind the chairs stretch their arms and hands above the heads of the sitters. It looks strange to you, but somehow natural and comforting. The aura of the room is loving — something you're not used to.

You wish your mother were here—to feel the energy. You wish the whole world could feel this peaceful. You decide to go sit in one of the chairs and experience what happens.

As the man behind your chair lifts his arms, you feel an instant warmth. For a moment, you are fearful. The feeling is strange and you don't understand it. You want to get up and run.

Slowly, your fear diminishes as you begin feeling warm. You enjoy the temperature shift. An energy surrounds you that is more loving than anything you've ever known.

All too soon, you return to your seat. You want more. The music swells and your heart does, too. Time passes and you realize you have been sitting quietly for over an hour without any pain. You smile, and for once, don't want to analyze. You decide not to interfere with your body feeling good with mind talk.

Time passes and the faith healing session ends. Slowly you leave the room, not wanting to let go of the loving energy.

You want to know more so you decide to attend a lecture on faith healing.

The speaker begins, "Myrtle Fillmore, cofounder of the Unity religion, was dying of TB, when she attended her first faith healing service. She'd heard about self-healing, self-trust, listening to what her body wanted. She healed herself and lived to be a very old woman.

"What she did, you can do, too. Faith healing isn't abandoning traditional medical treatment. It is an amendment, an added dividend to help the healing of your body.

"You've all heard stories of the doctor giving the patient three months to live. The patient dies on the exact date.

"You've also heard about people who defied their death sentences and outlived their doctors. Why do some people live full lives regardless of their medical problems?

"I suggest it might be due to faith in themselves and a strong mission.

"A woman was diagnosed with terminal throat cancer at age 30. The doctors said her cancer was inoperable. They predicted she only had six months to live.

"The woman had a Down's syndrome son and refused to die before him. She'd spent her life keeping her son out of an institution.

"I met her when she was 65. She still had throat cancer. Her son was still alive.

"There are many stories of such people who defy death. We don't know why some individuals die early and others don't. I do know that you will be happier and healthier believing in a higher power.

Faith healing is a way of connecting to your God Power.

"Carl G. Jung, the noted Swiss psychologist, spoke about a Universal Intelligence, where all information is to be found. All you have to do is 'tune in—tap out' your fears and limitations and connect with your faith and self-trust.

"Faith is accepting YOU. Trust is believing YOU."

The speaker finishes with a prayer. For the first time, you believe you can be healed.

✳

Medical Intuition gives you faith.

5

Listening to Your Body

THE SEMINAR IS OVER. It only lasted a few days, but you feel as if your whole life has changed. You feel optimistic. As the days pass, your enthusiasm lessens. Your fears returns and so do your pains.

Weeks go by as you go deeper into depression. "No one can help me. I was only kidding myself at the healing service. The speakers were taking advantage of us. They just wanted our $10." You doubt all the good you felt during the healing seminar. Your anger mounts as your fears enfold you.

In desperation, you pray for a miracle.

The phone rings. It's your friend calling to ask, "I've just discovered a study group that teaches how to develop your intuition. Are you interested?"

You look up at the sky and say thanks.

Your first group meeting is scary, exciting,

"The thoughts that come often unsought, and, as it were, drop into the mind, are commonly the most valuable of any we have."

—JOHN LOCKE, LETTERS TO SAMUEL BOLD, MAY 16, 1699

wondrous. You meet the other members and discover you are the only beginner. The others have been reading and studying ESP for over twenty years.

The leader is a woman in her early 40s, dark, slim, attractive. She says, "The purpose of this group is to experiment and experience how you can increase your intuitive skills. Each time we meet, we will do an ESP experiment.

"Today's experiment is to hold the watch of another person in the group. As you hold the watch, pay attention to your thoughts and notice any temperature shifts in your hands."

You accept the watch of one of the other women and hold it in your left hand, per the leader's instruction, "The left hand is the receiver, the right hand is the sender."

You don't notice anything different for a few seconds. Suddenly the watch gets so hot your hand feels like it is on fire. You drop the watch like a hot potato.

Fear takes over. "Did I do something evil? Why did the watch burn me? Am I going against my religion by participating in this exercise?"

The leader interrupts your thoughts, "Why did you react so strongly to the watch?"

"I don't know. I felt like my hand was going to burn up!"

The leader lowers her voice and says, "Close your eyes and answer my questions as quickly as you can. Don't analyze. Just let the answers come from your intuition."

"I don't want to do this," I say.

"Trust me. I'm going to help you."

Her voice is comforting, but I am afraid. I don't know what else to do, so I nod yes.

"Go back to the burning feeling. Was any other place in your body feeling like it was burning up?"

My voice shakes as I say, "I wasn't aware of any other hot spots in my body."

"Close your eyes. Remember how hot the watch felt. Don't let go of the feeling. Scan your body with your mind."

Your mind reacts instantly. First your hand burns, then you realize your chest and stomach are also burning. "Here," you point to your stomach.

"Good," she says. "Now ask your stomach why it reacted so strongly?"

You smile and think, she must be kidding. "Talk to my stomach? How?"

"Pretend," she says, "that your stomach is an old friend. Just ask it why it is burning?"

You feel stupid, but can't think how to get out of this. You imagine a small person in your stomach talking. To your amazement, you hear a voice saying, "Temper. . . hot over job . . . need to cool down."

You look at the owner of the watch thinking she had said the words to you. She looks shocked. She asks, "How did you know that?"

"I don't know. I didn't even know I'd said the words aloud." Your voice and hands are trembling. You don't want to play anymore. Fear takes over. This isn't a game.

The leader senses your fear and says, "Most people are afraid of their intuition. It represents the unknown, the dark of the night. Fear sets in because they can't explain how they arrived at their insights. Don't be afraid. Trust your instincts."

Another member of the group explains, "When my mother got sick from cancer, she couldn't shut down her fears. I taught her hypnosis to reduce her anxieties, but she was afraid of losing control of her mind."

The leader says, "There is the same concern in intuitive development."

A third member jumps in excitedly. "I've been 'tuning' into how many letters will be in the mail every day. I get scared when I'm right. Why?"

The leader responds, "It's frightening to open doors that we closed because we don't know how we know something.

"One young student had a intuitive flash that her father would die in a plane crash. When he died in a place crash, she thought it was her fault and she got very ill. Medical Intuition helped her let go of her guilt and the pains in her head.

"You're here to discover how to trust what you feel and find ways to validate your hunches."

❋

Medical Intuition means listening to what your body is trying to tell you.

6

Identifying Fear

THE GROUP EXPERIMENTS WERE exciting, but not always positive. One week our group attended another intuitive development group.

Everyone sat around a large boardroom table while their leader, a large, tall, imposing woman, sat at the head of the table and led us into a meditation.

Her voice wasn't pleasant. You tried not to think and just relax, but you couldn't. Your heart began to beat too fast. Your chest felt like someone was crushing it. You couldn't breathe. Something was wrong, but you couldn't speak or move.

"The only thing we have to fear is fear itself."
—FRANKLIN DELANO ROOSEVELT

Terror consumed you. You envisioned a dark, evil force taking over your body.

The woman next to you shouts out, "Turn up the lights. We need to help this person." She was pointing to me.

She shouts my name. "Open your eyes. Look at me," she yells.

You open your eyes and see their group leader. She is smiling, enjoying your pain. You know in that instant that she is the evil force. Your breath is labored and you feel faint.

Your friends lift you out of your chair, guiding you out of the room where the air feels lighter. Your legs are shaky, but soon you begin breathing normally. When you're back to normal, your friends suggest going for coffee.

At the restaurant, your group leader says, "You need to learn how to protect yourself from psychic vampirism."

"I don't understand."

She explains, "Psychic vampirism is when another person possesses your energy field and drains it.

"Consider watching famous people on television. You laugh when others laugh because it's contagious. If the story line is scary, you may get caught up in fear and not sleep well.

"The more sensitive you are, the more you will absorb the energies of others. You can get a headache just listening to people who complain a lot.

"I remember one incident when I woke up feeling great. Sixty seconds later, I was filled with fear and didn't know why. That terrible fear didn't lessen until my daughter called from a hospital to tell me about her car accident.

"Then I realized I had been intuitively absorbing her fear and pain. Once I understood what had happened, I was able to release the negative feelings.

"If I'd remembered to protect my energy field, I would have been able to tune in to my fears and 'know' who or what was causing them.

"You need to learn how to put a safety shield around your energy field so that what happened tonight doesn't happen again.

"Try this exercise:

"1. Don't assume the fear is always yours. Check it out.

"2. Ask who or what is causing your terror?

"3. Ask your inner intuitive, why this person is having fear?

"4. If you can help, do it. Otherwise, let go and let God take over."

It's too much to think about. You just want to go home. You try to stand but your legs are still wobbly. All you can think about is the ugly, evil woman, the leader of the other group.

✳

Medical Intuition means identifying the fear.

CHAPTER

7

Why You Get Sick

ALL WEEK LONG YOU VACILLATE, "Should I go back or should I quit?" You decide to attend one more time. "If I'm scared again, I'm out," you say to yourself.

The leader begins, "Tonight we're going to see how easily you absorb the pain of others.

"Pick a partner and sit directly opposite each other. Hold hands and close your eyes. Note any feelings or thoughts you have. Trust your instincts."

The last words resonate in your body. "Trust my instincts?" You want to stand up and scream, angrier than you've ever gotten.

"The pain of the mind is worse than the pain of the body."
—PUBLILIUS SYRUS

Your partner yells out, "Trust my instincts? Are you crazy? Whenever I do that, I get into trouble."

Her hands feel slimy and burning. You release them instantly.

"Stop yelling," you want to say, but don't. Her anger is consuming you.

"I've got to get away," but before you can get up, you begin visualizing an old memory.

You're 5 years old. Your brother is yelling at your mother, "I'll kill you. I hate you."

She is holding your hand tight. She is furious. You can feel her stomach boiling.

Your stomach starts boiling, too. You don't like the feeling, but don't know what to do.

The vision fades and you return to the present.

Your partner has finally quieted down, but you know she is still irate. Your stomach is hot and now it's in pain.

The leader says, "Tell your partner what you felt, sensed."

You panic. "Tell what I experienced? No way! All my life my imagination has gotten me into trouble. I'm not going to be made fun of, or thought crazy." You press your lips tight.

"Take a chance," says the leader. "Pretend you're telling a bedtime story to a child. Just make it all up."

The idea of making up a story lessens your apprehensions. You decide to make up a story and not tell it the way it happened. You begin...

"I saw you as a little child being held tightly by your mother. She was very angry and you wanted to get away, but you couldn't. You got scared and your stomach hurt."

Your partner's eyes fly wide open. "That's incredible. You tapped into my childhood. My mother was always angry, always trying to whip me. I still have stomachaches from her beatings."

"Do you have a brother?" you ask.

"Yes. He gives me headaches, always getting into trouble."

You're confused. Why did you get a scene from your childhood when it was your partner who had the problem?

As if reading your mind, the leader says, "You get the information the best way your mind can assimilate it. You're a visual person, one who can 'see' the pain of others. Other members of this group use other senses."

Another member said, "That's why I felt my partner's pain in my forehead? I thought the pain was mine."

"I heard what was wrong with my partner. I thought she actually told me the information," said another woman.

The leader says, "We feel things first. Later we try to understand. Confusion comes when we interrupt the intuitive and try to make it fit into some logic that we can accept.

"I believe many of you take on the illnesses of others and the doctors call it psychosomatic."

You bolt upright. All your life you have been labeled psychosomatic.

✳

Medical Intuition helps you understand why you get sick.

8

Understanding Your Past

ONE YEAR HAS PASSED SINCE you attended your first Medical Intuition conference. You still have pains throughout your body. Your health has not improved. You ponder what to do next.

Your friend calls. "Want to attend another Medical Intuition conference?"

"Yes," you answer quickly.

"Wellness depends on how fully you understand your body's reaction to people, places, and things," the speaker says. "To heal your body, you need to identify those patterns.

"For instance, you might be overly sensitive to others. You may feel their pains so acutely, that your body hurts when they hurt.

"Imagine a friend looking tired. Your sensitivity picks up his or her weakness. You have a choice.

Coincidence: a striking occurrence of two or more events at one time apparently by mere chance.

—WEBSTER'S ENCYCLOPEDIC UNABRIDGED DICTIONARY, 1994

You can absorb the sick energies or use your sensitivity to help.

"There are no coincidences, only growth lessons.

"Illness occurs when you take on someone's pain, knowingly or unknowingly. Your body will react in a pattern you have created.

"Today's lesson is to write about all the memorable experiences in your life and search for the reactor patterns."

You raise your hand and ask, "I'm too old to remember every year. What do I do?"

The speaker laughs and says, "Record the years you do remember; a death, a birth, the year of your marriage, your divorce, a special award, etc.

"Let your feelings come first. You probably won't have enough time to finish this project today, so write as much as you can. Realize your past holds all the information on how you handle pain, love, fear, joy."

You began to write your history.

Age .... experience .... result ....

6 months: dog licks my face, get an infection. Hover between life and death for 3 days.

5 years: neighbor's watchdog chases me up a flight of stairs and tears the screen on the outside

door, trying to bite me. Nightmares begin: always a large dog chasing me, trying to destroy me.

8 years: have to repeat third grade, humiliated, embarrassed. Feel unloved and stupid.

9 years: nightmares begin after death of grandmother.

12 years: hate school — feel isolated. Can't sleep.

19 years: marry wrong partner; too young to know better.

20 years: first child born with birth defect. Cosmetic surgery fixes it.

22 years: second child born with multiple birth defects. All corrected. Spouse unable to deal with medical problems.

24 years: third child born normal. Hooray!

25 years: spouse mentally ill. Verbally abusive. I want out of marriage, but don't want the world to know I failed.

26 years: car hits my car. I get whiplash bad.

27 years: another car hits my car. Whiplash pains more severe.

29 years: third car accident. Wonder why I keep getting hit from behind? Whiplash pains never let up.

30 years: fourth car accident again in April. What is God trying to tell me? Whiplash pains severe.

31 years: mother is dying of leukemia. Marriage is dying. Another car hits my car in April. Think I'd better stop driving from April 1st—30th.

32 years: mother dies, so does my marriage. This time my fifth car accident happens in February. Whiplash pain horrible.

34 years: meet soulmate. Get married. Life is wonderful.

36 years: another car hits me from behind. Accidents always happen at stoplights, stop signs. Begin having ailments that no one can explain.

37 years: ailments increasing in intensity. Side effects of medicine worse than illness. Stopped taking medications. Choose to have only one ailment at a time.

38 years: ailments have escalated to incurable disease. Allergic to medications. Doctors suggest moving to different climate.

40 years: join national spiritual group. Attend first faith healing session. Want to be healed.

41 years: join study group to increase intuitive skills. Start to trust my instincts more.

42 years: have session with Medical Intuitive who "sees" how to help me find the right medical treatment.

The speaker interrupts. "This is a lifetime project. Don't worry if you can't finish it all today. Keep searching for the words that keep repeating: happy, sad, lacking, loss, success. You'll begin to see your pattern."

Your most common patterns are:

Fear of animals, nightmares, loss of sleep, car accidents that always happen from behind, divorce, remarriage.

Illnesses—pains—medicines that don't help; divorce doesn't change sick patterns, intuitive training helps.

You wonder why so many car accidents?

You wonder why the car accidents happened mostly in April?

You wonder if somehow you could have avoided the accidents?

You begin to understand why you've had insomnia, but still don't know what to do about it.

Despair sets in as you realize you have spent most of your life waiting.

✳

Medical Intuition means understanding your past.

CHAPTER

9

Trusting Your Creativity

THE SPEAKER INTERRUPTS YOUR THOUGHTS, "Many of you have been asking yourselves, Who am I? What will I be when I grow up? In our next session, you'll have the opportunity to get some of those questions answered.

"*Imaginaton is not a talent of some men, but is the health of every man.*"
—RALPH WALDO EMERSON

"Pick a partner and share your life story. You'll have five minutes to talk and then your partner will give you feedback on how he or she views your strengths."

Your partner is a young, thin man, who is graying at the temples. He starts by saying, "I've always been sensitive. My father wants me to be just like him, strong, and a macho machine. He always said I was too sensitive. I can't please him and like me at the same time.

"Several years ago I developed a lung problem. The doctors say there is no cure. Most of the time I feel like someone is sitting on my chest. The prognosis is that I'll get so sick, I'll die.

"I'm married to a wonderful woman. I'm lucky to have her. I wonder why she stays with me.

"I've always wanted to be a writer, but my father said I needed a reliable career. So I sell insurance like him. I'm a good salesman. I really like helping people.

"I'm not sure why I came here today. I don't know what I'm going to do." His eyes had large red circles, his skin was pale and discolored with yellow spots. Your heart wrenches in sympathy for his pain.

"Tell your partner what you perceived as his or her strengths," says the speaker.

Your throat tightens. What can you say that will offer some hope to this man, a stranger who is being more intimate with you than your closest friend?

You pray for guidance. "Make up a story," you hear from inside your head. Your heart opens and you hear yourself saying, "If you don't mind, I'd like to make up a fairy tale about you."

The man shrugs his shoulders. He knows nothing good is going to happen. It's the story of his life. "Sure. Go ahead."

"Once upon a time there was a king that wanted his son to learn how to be the best ruler. The king was old and knew soon his son would have to take over.

"The prince didn't want to be a king. He only wanted to sing and play his mandolin.

The king said, 'You play the mandolin well, but you need to learn how to rule wisely. You will have to spend all your time learning and reading about kingdomship.'

"The prince tried to learn, but all he wanted to do was play his mandolin.

"One day the prince fell in love with the beautiful princess from the next country. They married and had two beautiful children. The prince often composed songs on his mandolin to make the children merry.

"The years went by and the king grew very old and sick. The prince knew soon he would have to rule the kingdom. He became fearful. 'I'm not my father. He is a good king. I just want to play the mandolin and make people happy.'

"The king dies and the people proclaim the prince as the new king. Day after day, the prince tries to be just like his father. But alas, he couldn't continue to pretend to be something he wasn't.

"His beautiful and wise wife said, 'Play the mandolin for your people. Let them hear the beauty that lies within your heart. When you must decide for others, compose a song that answers the question.'

"The prince liked what his wife advised. Soon he was known all over the land for his music and ability to arbitrate disputes. Angry people became trans-

*formed — willing to resolve differences. Never before
in history had this kingdom been so prosperous.*

"You are like that prince. You have the ability to
make people happy," you say to your partner. "Do it
your way. Sell insurance as if you were an actor
playing a part. The purpose of the play is to help the
audience understand what they need to know. Be the
writer, the director and the producer. Do it your
way."

The man sits straight, tears flowing. "Thank
you," he says. "Now I know why I came today." He
reaches out his arms and we hug.

"Your turn," he says.

✳

Medical Intuition means trusting your creativity.

CHAPTER

10

Believing in Your Future

"ALL MY LIFE I'VE WANTED TO BE famous, which doesn't make sense because I like my privacy. When I was young, I pretended the 'Millionaire' from the TV show would come knocking on my door to give me a million dollars tax free.

"Just as our eyes need light in order to see, our minds need ideas in order to conceived."

—NICOLAS MALEBRANCHE

"The money would help me get the proper training to learn to speak well. The millionaire never knocked on my door and I was so shy, I found it difficult to speak in public.

"I'm a middle child and my two siblings got all the verbal skills. I had to work harder most of the time.

"I'm married, have two children, a boy and a girl, who are incredible individuals. My son is a national speaker for a well-known company, and my daughter is a psychologist.

"My spouse has a career that pays well and here I am, still waiting for the millionaire to come knocking."

The speaker interrupts. "It's time for your partner to talk about your strengths."

The man swallows hard. "I don't think I can do this as well as you, but here goes.

"When you were talking, I kept hearing the word 'trapped,' and it made me think of a fish who wanted to be a bird.

"The fish kept swimming to the surface of the water to watch the birds. He envied them and often thought, 'If only I had been born with wings. I'd be free to soar through the skies. I'd fly anywhere in the world. No one, nothing could stop me from living my life the way I wanted to.'

"But alas the fish was only a fish!

"One day the fish saw a man with a fishing pole pull one of his friends out of the water. He knew from past experiences he'd never see his friend again. He swam as fast as he could to get away. He swam further than he'd ever gone before.

"The water grew colder. He saw new and different types of fish. He looked up and saw a shoreline filled with sand and seashells.

"He got so excited. He was free at last. It didn't matter if he was a bird or not. He could discover the world his way."

My partner said, "I kept thinking you feel trapped in your life and I wondered if you have a lot of pain in your body?" You nod yes.

"I don't know you very well, but I think you've got a wild imagination. Why don't you write stories for children? Use your creativity to see the world in a fresh, new way.

"You helped me. Now help yourself get out of your rut. Be your best friend. It's only your self-imposed limits that stop you. I see you as someone who could be famous for storytelling."

Your heart beats faster. Could I be a famous storyteller? You're unaware that your pain is gone.

The teacher interrupts, "Sorry folks. It's time to bring this session to a close."

You leave wishing there had been more time.

✳

Medical Intuition means believing in your dreams.

11

Releasing the Pain of the Past

YOUR SLEEP IS DISTURBED BY a nightmare. All you can remember about the dream is a helpless feeling of being trapped.

Your body is racked with pain. You're tired of hurting. You try to sleep but an old memory returns to haunt you.

You're 3 years old. You've just picked up a vase on the dining room table. It was too heavy. You dropped the vase and it broke. The vase was an heirloom.

> *"A bodily disease may be but a symptom of some ailment in the spiritual past."*
> —NATHANIEL HAWTHORNE

Your mother heard the noise and ran into the dining room, where you sat in the middle of the broken pieces of glass. She hurt your arm as she yanked you out of the debris. Her anger kept her from noticing the blood on your arm.

"You bad boy. Stay in your room and don't move until your dad gets home to punish you." Then she closed the lights and the door.

It was dark and you were afraid. You couldn't fight her. You didn't know what to do, and you still don't. In spite of your age, she still scares you and you still feel like that frightened little child. "

The next day, you told the speaker about your nightmare and childhood memory. "Why does it still bother me?" you asked.

"You learn most of your beliefs from the people who raise you. They want you to believe their way. When you don't, they try to convince you otherwise.

"Your mother may not have realized what she was doing to you when she made your bedroom a terrifying place.

"My concern is that you are still feeling trapped and afraid. Would you be willing to be a guinea pig at my workshop today?" I nod yes.

She places two chairs opposite one another and motions for you to sit in one.

"Learning how to communicate with the most difficult people in our lives is our lesson for today.

"We have a volunteer who broke an heirloom vase at age 3. The child's punishment was to be locked in a dark bedroom for a long time. To this day, the mother's temperament still causes the volunteer fear and pain."

She turns to you and says, "Pretend your mother is sitting in the empty chair opposite you. Tell her how angry you are about being locked in your bedroom when you were only 3 years old. Speak like a child."

You're nervous. You've never like being the center of attention, but you want to get rid of your disease.

"Mother. You shouldn't have locked me in the dark. I'm sorry for breaking your vase. I didn't want it to break."

The teacher says, "Change chairs. Be your mother."

"You were warned not to touch things that don't belong to you. You were a bad boy and you deserved to be punished. I'm not sorry I locked you in your room."

You are told to change chairs again.

"You're a mean lady. You don't love me and I don't love you either."

When you switched chairs, you imagine your mother speaking in a softer tone, "You don't mean that. You know I love you."

Sharp, shooting pains enter your body. The pains are so severe, you don't know if you can continue. The teacher touches your shoulder gently and nods for you to go on.

Back in your chair, "You say you love me, but

you don't. All you ever wanted was your precious things. You shouldn't have been a mother. You're mean and evil."

You are told to switch chairs again, and take on your mother's energy. You begin to feel her fears and hear her thoughts, "I was never taught how to love. I thought loving was being tough. I put you in a dark room. so you'd learn to be strong."

Fascinated by your new insight, you automatically move back to your chair and speak to the group without seeing their faces. "I never knew my mother was afraid. I always thought she was ready to do battle with the world. I thought she was tough, but she wasn't—isn't."

Your body stops hurting.

The teacher explains, "My Medical Intuition tells me your pains began when you were locked in that dark room. In your need for love, you unconsciously absorbed your mother's fears.

"I'm not sure if you can accept what I'm going to say now. Realize that as a child, your energy field was wide open to all the emotions and fears of your mother. You didn't know how to protect your energy field. You just wanted her to stop hurting. When you couldn't handle her emotions, you got sick.

"I saw your hands covering your stomach when you were first imagining talking to your mother. When you had your sudden insight, your hands released your stomach and you sat straighter. You mastered the first step in learning how to separate your mother's fears from yours.

"Keep doing this type of role-playing for the next 14 days. The more you know about your mother's fears, the more you can let go of the physical pains that aren't yours."

✳

Medical Intuition helps you release the pains of the past.

12

Understanding Your Dreams

Y OU'RE THINKING THE NEXT time you have a meeting with your mother, you'll be less concerned about her approval. Instead of dreading the visit, you're looking forward to it.

You fall asleep and dream about the home you lived in as a small child.

You're standing in front of your home. You observe an oversized swing set in the front yard of one of the houses down the street. The swing set is so big you wonder who plays on it and why is it in the front yard? You think that's so unusual.

> *"The biggest disease today is not Leprosy or Tuberculosis, but rather the feeling of not being wanted."*
>
> —MOTHER TERESA

You see two large men in a car driving slowly by your house. You think you know them, so you wave hello, but they don't stop. They drive around the block toward the back of your home.

You run to get closer to the car, and realize the men weren't who you thought they were.

One of the men grabs you and a struggle ensues. When you realize you're not strong enough to fight the man, you stop resisting. The man loosens his grip and you seize the opportunity to get away.

You run into your home screaming for help. Your father hears your call, sees the man chasing you and tackles him to the floor. The police come and arrest the two men.

You awake frightened, wondering why you dreamt about your old home, the oversized swing set and why the man was chasing you.

Same night: the next dream.

You go upstairs to your old bedroom and discover nothing is the same. Your toys, clothes, and books have all been thrown carelessly into the closet. It's a mess.

Someone is lying in your bed. You call the person by name, but it's not who you think it is.

Your ex-spouse helps you take the pictures down from the wall. Afterward, the walls change to brick. You have a sense of life starting over.

Your sister walks in with her husband, who is now fully recovered and happy.

You walk back into your old bedroom and everything is neater and back where it belonged.

You awake feeling great, wondering what the two dreams meant.

The conference is over. You think about your options: consult your therapist, try to interpret the dreams yourself, or have a one-on-one Medical Intuitive consultation.

The MIC asks: "Oversized swing set, mistaken identities, fear, pain. What do those terms represent in your present life?"

You: "My disease. I'm terrified I'll die in excruciating pain. I pray the doctors are wrong about my prognosis."

MIC: "What was it like living in your old home?"

You: "Safe, friendly, my father was always there to protect me. I wasn't sick then."

MIC: "You had similarities in both dreams. Mistaken identities of people you thought you knew. The man in the car in the first dream, and the person lying on your bed in the second dream. Do you generally jump to fast decisions about people, only to discover they're not who or what you thought they were?"

You: "When I meet someone for the first time, I find people likable. When I discover the person isn't telling me the truth, I get disappointed and then I feel pain. Oh my God! I'm acting just like my mother. Finding faults with the people I like. That hurts."

MIC: "Bingo! Now let's see what else your dreams were telling you. Bedrooms can represent many things: an oasis, a place to be yourself, a rest-ing spot, etc. Were you at all upset that someone was lying on your bed?"

You: "No. I was just wondering why that per-son was there."

MIC: "Was she or he healthy?"

You: "I think so."

MIC: "Could that person represent the old, healthy you?"

You: "Maybe. I'm not sure."

MIC: "Your bedroom was changed. Your pos-sessions tossed carelessly in the closet. A stranger is lying on your bed and you're not getting upset. Why not?"

You: "I didn't like my things being touched and discarded as if they meant nothing. I was trying to figure it out rather than get angry about the changes."

MIC: "Do you ever mentally hide your body inside a closet because it's too messy or too painful?"

You: "Sort of," as your head bobs down.

MIC: "I'd like to give you my interpretation of your dreams and then ask for feedback, if that's all right with you?" You nod yes again.

"I remember seeing you last year at this confer-ence. You didn't walk as straight as today. Are you feeling better?"

You: "Yes. In fact I made an appointment with my doctor for later today. I think he's going to be surprised at my recovery."

MIC: "Your disease is giving you mixed messages. The oversized swing set may be how you view your condition. It's so large, how can anyone play with it?

"Your pains are too big for you. They don't belong where everyone can see them in the front yard.

"The man chasing you may represent your fear of pain. He is the unknown. You thought you knew who he was, but you were mistaken. You've attended the Medical Intuition seminar to help you get well, but your body is still in pain.

"I'm particularly impressed by your sister's husband walking healthy and happy. Can you explain more about your brother-in-law?"

You: "Yes. He's had an incurable bout with lupus. The doctors think he only has a few more years. He's in pain most of the time."

MIC: "So, seeing him healthy and well gives you hope. Think of your sister and brother-in-law as two aspects of you, representing healing and loving support. Often in dreams, your mind sees you well before your body changes.

"It sounds like your dreams are giving you hopeful messages of changes for the better. In both dreams you're getting help and things improve.

"Consider joining a Medical Intuition study group in your area to help you stay focused on your healing."

✳

Medical Intuition means understanding your dreams.

CHAPTER

13

Seeing Clearly

YOUR DOCTOR'S APPOINTMENT was a BIG disappointment. He said, "I'm sorry, but your health prognosis hasn't changed."

You say, "I can't believe it. I've been doing so much visualization, meditation, and faith healing. How can there be no change?" The doctor smiles kindly and shrugs his shoulders.

"One starts an action, simply because one must do something."

—T. S. ELIOT, THE ELDER STATESMAN, 1958

You leave his office in a daze and walk across a busy street hoping a car will hit you and end all your misery.

Anger rises. "I won't let the doctors be right. I will get well. I'll show them."

Your shoulders slump as you think, "They don't care. No one cares if I live or die. I wish I were dead." You're tired and your body hurts.

You sit on a park bench and look around. There are birds flying back and forth, children playing nearby. The sun is warm and the sky is blue.

You sit for awhile and let the sun beat its rays on your body now racking with pain. Later you walk slowly back home.

The phone rings. It's your friend asking if you want to attend a Medical Intuition study group.

"Medical Intuition is a journey into self-healing," said the MI instructor. "It's a way of discovering what and who might be at the core of your disease.

"Many of you are here because you can't find any answers to your health problems. You have pains the doctors can't explain. You're frustrated, angry and sometimes depressed.

"Tonight you'll learn how past lives may influence your present health condition.

"Seven years ago I had severe eye problems: cataracts, glaucoma, optic nerve damage. I was labeled 'visually impaired.' Most people are 20-20. I was 20-400.

"I learned to read Braille with my fingers, walked with a white cane, and was feeling pretty sorry for myself most of the time.

"My worse problem was I was ridden with fear that my 10-year-old daughter would be brutally killed.

"I often said, I don't want to see her hurt. I'd check her limbs daily to see if they were intact. I never had any logical reasons for my fears until I had my Siberia past life recall.

Past life: Two men and I were trying to get some friends out of prison that we felt were wrongly incarcerated. We were enthusiastic about helping them, but didn't have a plan.

The Russian soldiers caught us and decided to make us a big example.

They took my 3-year-old daughter, tied her limbs to four horses and when the gun was shot, her body was ripped apart.

I was so shocked by this, I screamed, "I can't look at this." In my horror, I pulled my eyes out of my head and went insane. I died shortly afterward, consumed with guilt.

"You may not believe in past lives. You may think I was imagining the whole thing. It doesn't matter.

"Since I had that past life recall, I don't fear my daughter being brutally murdered anymore.

"I started eye exercises, positive thinking, and visualization to change my old mental messages to my eyes.

"Past life understanding helped me 'see' clearly."

✳

Medical Intuition helps you see clearly.

14

Transforming Fears

ONE OF THE OTHER GROUP members tells her story.

"I've had insomnia most of my life. There are nights when I only get one or two hours of broken sleep. I envy people who sleep an entire night without waking.

"When I was a teenager, my family was poor, and we lived in the back of a store. The basement had a huge hill of dirt where dozens of large rats lived. At night, I'd hear them moving and scratching. Those sounds terrified me.

> *"Night brings our troubles to the light, rather than banishes them."*
> —SENECA, LETTERS TO LUCILIUS (1ST C.), 56.6

"My brother added to my fears when he teasingly told me his birthmark was from a rat biting him in his crib.

"One day I was taking a bath, I just happened to look over the side of the tub by the wall. There was a huge hole that hadn't been there before. We knew the only animal that could have created the hole had to be a rat.

"My father plastered the hole and covered it with chicken wire. A few nights later, I woke up and saw a large rat staring at me from the doorway. I screamed and woke my parents. The rat ran away. My father immediately poured rat poison in all the corners of the rooms.

"A week later I saw the rat laying on my pillow dying. I screamed and screamed as the rat slowly walked off my bed.

"I never saw that rat again so I don't know if it died inside our home or elsewhere, but the fear of it returning haunted me until my recent past life awakening.

"A few months later, I was trying to sleep in a room in Phoenix, Arizona, far away from home. It was so hot the hotel keeper had given me a fan to cool the room. The fan was blowing some papers around my room. I didn't want to shut off the fan, but the sounds of the rustling papers scared me.

"I looked at the open doorway and saw a large, ugly rat. I knew it was only my imagination because I could see through the rat as if it was a sheer, filmy fabric.

"My imagination said the rat was hungry and wanted food. I kept telling myself I was only imagining the rat. My mind was rational, but my fears weren't. I got up and left the room.

"I sat at the top of the stairwell hoping someone would come out of their room and talk to me. I wanted to scream, but since I knew it was only my imagination, I stopped myself from waking the other people in the house.

"My fears heightened and in my imagination I saw dozens of large, ugly rats coming up the stairs. I labeled them King Rats, because they were so big.

"My inner mind told me they were hungry, and that I represented food. They were going to eat me.

"I'd been working with past life regressions for many years to overcome my fear of animals. The only phobia left was my fear of rats.

"I wasn't surprised when my intuition said, 'This is a past life you need to work through.'

"I decided to allow my past life to surface."

Past life: I saw myself as the only healthy sailor on a sailing ship. All my shipmates had died or were dying from a disease the rats had infected them with. Now the rats were eating them, dead or alive.

I kept trying to steer the ship to land, but land was far away. The rats were eating anything that smelled. They kept coming up the two stairwells on either side of me. As long as I made noises and stayed alert, they backed off. When I was quiet, they'd return.

*Days went by and no land was in sight. I was so
exhausted, I finally fell asleep.*

*I was awakened by intense pain. I opened my eyes
and found myself lying on the floor of the deck. The
rats were eating my flesh and one was about to take
a chunk out of my face. I saw the rat's face clearly
before he began eating my chin.*

*Death didn't come easy. I was being eaten alive
and the pain and fear were horrendous.*

"When I returned to the present, I realized I had had
a tremendous breakthrough. I finally knew why I
was such a poor sleeper. I was always on guard at
night, listening for sounds.

"In the morning I made an appointment with a
past life regressionist who helped me go further to
understand.

"He suggested I do a Gestalt exercise with the
rat who died on my bed. Usually I enjoy role-playing, but not this time. Talking to a rat was not high
on my list of things to do.

"Insomnia had plagued me most of my life. I
was willing to try anything to get a good night's sleep.

"I felt crazy talking to an imaginary rat, but I
knew I needed to understand my rat connection.

"He put two chairs opposite each other. I was to
imagine the rat sitting in one of the chairs talking to
me."

"The rat spoke. 'I don't like being a rat. I want to be like you, a human being. I like you because you always know when I'm around, even though you don't hear me. You're nice and clean. None of my family are clean. They enjoy filth. I don't. What I don't understand is your fear of me.'"

"I began to think, 'The rat isn't any different than me. I wasn't happy with who I was either. I'm just not as ugly.'

"The rat and I discussed how we each used our senses to survive. I almost began to like the rat, but not enough to keep him around.

"With the therapist's guidance, I told the rat he had to leave. I was sorry, but I didn't want him as a friend. The rat finally understood. He wanted to live a different life, but couldn't. Sadly, he left my life forever.

"Since then, I've been able to sleep peacefully without fear. Half a century of insomnia was cured by recalling and working with a Gestalt therapist on a past life.

"I bless that therapist for helping me and not ridiculing my past life recall. I overcame a major problem and so can you. Don't be afraid of your fears. Use them as tools to help you transform your fears."

Medical Intuition helps you transform your fears.

15

Letting Go of Pain

ALL NIGHT LONG, YOU TOSS AND TURN until your blanket and sheet are in a knot. You wake and say aloud, "Fine, now my blanket has me trapped."

You try to rid the "trapped" thoughts from your mind, but you can't. Getting sick is a way of keeping you trapped. You're trapped in your job and in your life. You're stuck.

In the morning, you call a MIC to rid your trapped thoughts.

*"Great thoughts
reduced to
practice become
great acts."*
—WILLIAM HAZLITT

MIC: "Pay attention when a thought consumes you. Your intuitive scanner is constantly on the alert to notify you of opportunities of trouble ahead. It picks up signals all around you. When you listen, you get vital information. When you don't listen, you sabotage your success.

"When I was little, my mother was jealous of my friends. I wasn't aware of her jealousy. I didn't know she lacked self-confidence.

"When she said, 'Your best friend is taking advantage of you,' I believed my mother and I stopped trusting my friend. I didn't check my mother's reasoning, I just accepted her words as the whole truth.

"Whenever my mother said bad things about my friends, I'd get stomachaches. If I challenged her, she'd say I didn't love her. I had lots of stomachaches.

"My stomachaches continued throughout my childhood, whenever my mother would speak against someone I really liked, I'd hear my mind denying, 'She's wrong.' I'd think, 'My friend is a good person.' But my mother couldn't be wrong. I grew up distrusting people and doubting myself. The pains got worse.

"When my mother passed on, I thought my best friend had died. I still didn't trust me. My stomach pains got so severe my doctor suggested I consult a psychologist.

"In therapy, I uncovered the truth about my mother's jealousy. At first I denied our relationship wasn't perfect. I'd always put my mother on a pedestal. She wasn't just my mother, she was a saint.

"The truth hurt almost as much as the pains in my stomach. It took me three years of therapy to uncover the real story and value my thoughts. My therapist said, 'Listen to those recurring thoughts to know when someone is lying to you.' I learned that my stomach hurt whenever I denied the truth. I learned that my body had a built in scanner to warn me of danger. I learned to stop, look, and listen whenever my stomach hurt.

"The pains in my stomach occur only when I don't listen to what my body is trying to make me aware of. People watch the weather reports on TV to prepare for sudden changes of temperature. Listening to my thoughts prepares me for the unexpected.

"If you have a chronic ache in your body and no doctor seems to know why, listen to your thoughts.

"Medical Intuition training helped me to 'tune' into my body's messages. I'd like to share my method with you.

"1. You have an unrelenting thought going round and round in your mind.

"2. Say the thought aloud and be aware of where your body hurts: a sudden pain in the head, chest, stomach, back, etc.

"3. Define the pain(s): pressure, dull ache, throbbing, stabbing, etc.?

"4. Who does the pain remind you of?

"5. Let any thoughts about that person surface: sadness, joy . . .

"6. Think loving thoughts about this person: wellness, prosperity . . .

"7. Release the image and visualize your pain leaving your body like the smoke from a cigarette.

"8. Say an affirmation: 'I am free of pain. I am filled with the light. I am healthy.'

"9. Closing statement: 'Thank you . . . Amen . . . So be it!'

"Repeat the exercise as needed."

✳

Medical Intuition means letting go of pain.

16

Balancing Logic and Creativity

YOU CALL YOUR FRIEND. "Do you think our study group would like to learn Medical Intuition?"

"Yes! Yes! Yes!" she responds.

"Energy training is the basis of healing," begins our instructor. "Medical Intuition works through the five physical senses: smell, sight, sound, touch, taste, and feelings/intuition—the sixth sense."

"Energy: power, strength, vigor, vim, punch, go, dash, drive."
—THE NEW AMERICAN ROGET'S COLLEGE THESAURUS, 1958

One of our instructors, an electronics engineer, once said, "When you use only the five senses, you limit your mind. The sixth sense opens your mind to higher levels of intelligence and consciousness."

"Did you ever enter a building and feel uncomfortable, or dislike someone without knowing why?" The woman next to you bobs her head up and down like a bouncing ball.

"Most people sense, but few value their instincts enough to trust them. Everyone is born with a built-in energy scanner. Like the animals in the forest, you can sense danger, love, hunger, pain, and joy. Unlike the animals, most of you have been taught to ignore your basic instincts.

"Do any of you remember your mother placing her hand on your forehead to check for a temperature?" We nod yes.

"She was sensing your energy through her hand scanner. A hot or cold forehead would give your mother clues about your health. She was doing Medical Intuition through her touch.

"The body works like a computer. What you enter is what it believes. When that energy is disrupted by negative or positive input, the body listens and behaves accordingly.

"A woman who had back surgery lifted her 175 pound injured husband into her car to go to the nearest hospital.

"A doctor told his male patient he had only three months to live. He died exactly three months later.

"Energy is your birthright. No one can ever take it away unless you let them. Whenever you give your energy away, knowingly or unknowingly, the other person has more power over you.

"You are the captain of your body. How you direct your energy is your choice and only yours.

"Energy is power. Thomas Fuller said, 'The real difference between men is energy.'

"The body is divided into two energy fields. The right side represents the intuitive, creative, innovative aspects, whereas the left side represents logic, common sense, and experience. Often one side is more vigorous than the other. Do this exercise to discover which side of your body has the most energy.

"Breathe in and out ten times slowly and comfortably. Observe whether you inhale or exhale:

- More with the left or right nostril?
- Smoothly or roughly?

"If you inhale only through the left nostril, you tend to look at life from a more logical, intellectual position. If you inhale only through the right nostril, you tend to be more innovative.

"Balance in the mind and body occur when you inhale through both nostrils equally. A smooth inhalation indicates you accept new ideas easily. Individuals with bumpy inhalations are generally stubborn, strong willed and inflexible. The bumpier the inhalation, the more difficult it is for you to alter your beliefs.

"The exhalation represents how you let go of old ideas and negative emotions; smoothly or roughly.

"What you resist has power over your energy. Open your eyes and let's talk."

One of the men says, "I have a deviated septum. I can't breathe through one side. But in this exercise I found myself doing most of my breathing through the left side, where the problem is. Can you explain why?"

"This exercise deals with the energy of the mind. Anything is possible. Were you comfortable breathing this way?"

Student: "Yes. I found it easier, just confusing."

MIC: "Are you more logical than imaginative?"

Student: "Yes. I prefer knowing over guessing."

MIC: "There is no confusion. You are a person who is more grounded in logic than creativity. Often this happens when a person is involved in a project that demands a lot of research."

Student: "I am involved in a demanding project that requires a lot of research, but I can be creative, too."

MIC with a slight gleam in her eyes: "I am sure after you've exhausted your logic." The student's face turned red at the MIC's insight.

Student 2: "At first I was only able to inhale through the right side, but with concentration I was able to switch. What does that mean?"

MIC: "Excellent. Breathing only through the right side meant you were only utilizing a part of your energy. When you switched and used both nostrils, you balanced your thoughts and body.

Student 3: "I was breathing in smoothly through my left nostril and breathing out roughly through my right nostril. What does that mean?"

MIC: "It means you accept logical thoughts easily, but have a difficult time retaining creative input.

"Practice breathing through both nostrils equally and smoothly five minutes a day. This is a relaxation exercise for balancing your mind and body."

✳

Medical Intuition balances your logic with your creativity.

17

Finding Energy Blocks

"Medical Intuition requires an active imagination," began the MIC. "Imagine finding the perfect partner to spend the rest of your life with. Happy visions fuel the body with positive energy.

"When your imagination is in conflict with what is going on in your life, you have confusion, fear, and lack of self-trust.

"The next phase of Medical Intuition training requires you to allow your imagination to soar. No limits or fears. Don't deny whatever you perceive. Let go of your doubts and dare to dream great things.

> *"The quality of the imagination is to flow and not to freeze."*
> —RALPH WALDO EMERSON

"Close your eyes. Inhale through your mouth, and into your throat, chest, stomach, reproductive area and exhale through your toes.

"Bypass any area that restricts your breathing, but make a mental note to remember where the hindrance occurred. Imagine a tube going up your spine. Exhale into the tube and note where your breath gets stuck.

"Repeat this breathing exercise slowly six times and when you're done, open your eyes."

Student: "That was hard. I kept getting stuck in my throat."

MIC: "The throat area represents how you express your needs. If you have a difficult time expressing your feelings and wants, you may create a blockage there. Do you find yourself clearing your throat often?"

Student: "Yes, and no doctor has been able to help me."

MIC: "After you practice this exercise awhile, you may be able to alter that problem."

Student 2: "I had a similar problem with my chest. I imagined a large dark spot and never did breathe beyond that area. It scared me. I wondered if I had a tumor or something."

MIC, laughing: "Don't start jumping to conclusions. Medical Intuition is about locating energy blockages, not diagnosing illnesses. Viewing the dark cloud in your chest may mean you are lacking self-love, or you're smoking too much, or some issue from the past is blocking your growth. Can you relate to any of this?"

Student 2: "All of it. I just got divorced and my smoking is at an all-time high. I don't like being alone. I don't like my life right now."

Student 3: "I had the same reaction, but I'm happily married and I don't smoke."

MIC: "The heart area represents love. Often when individuals find a loving partner, she or he feels safe about letting old hurts surface."

Student 3's eyes flooded with tears.

MIC: "Limbs represent movement, action, stability, follow-through. Imagine getting a wonderful idea and getting weighed down with fears. Your legs may feel heavy, maybe even painful."

Student 5: "I invented something a few years ago, but couldn't see how to proceed. I don't know when my legs began hurting, but it may have been since then."

Student 6: "I tried to exhale up my spine. I couldn't. I felt like I had to exhale quickly through my open mouth."

MIC: "The lower spine represents how you carry the weight of your responsibilities, strong or weak. It also focuses on your lack of physical strength.

"The midriff and the mid-area of the spine contain any overly-stressful, emotional pain in your heart.

"The vertebrae closest to your neck represent the feeling of being pushed by others to do what you don't want to do."

Student 6: "I've listened to what you've been saying and it seems as if I have all the problems. I'm a mess."

MIC: "Energy blocks build like the layers of an ion. The more you give away your energy, the more physical problems you'll have in your body.

"Energy blocks are layers of fears, mixed messages and lack of self-trust. It takes time and understanding to identify the blocks and to know how to release them.

"The further people get from their energy, the more physical problems they will have in their bodies. Most people get energy problems long before the physical ailments manifest."

✳

Medical Intuition finds your energy blocks.

CHAPTER

18

Transforming Energy Blocks

"THE MORE YOU BECOME aware of your energy blocks, the more you will understand why some illnesses attach themselves to you," said the MIC.

"A woman with constant pains in her stomach went to many medical clinics and had dozens of tests. No doctor could find any reason for her pains. When her stomach pains occurred more often, she went to a psychologist for therapy, but nothing helped to reduced the pains.

"It wasn't until she learned about Medical Intuition that she realized how much her grandmothers' illnesses had frightened her. Both her grandmothers had died of colon ailments. Subconsciously she feared of dying the same horrible, painful death.

"She remembered her paternal grandmother dying in agonizing pain. She locked that memory in her colon. Her maternal grandmother lived in her

*"Sink in thyself!
There ask what
ails thee, at
that shrine!"*
—MATTHEW ARNOLD,
EMPEDOCLES ON ETNA
(1852) I.2

childhood home. She saw her in pain every day for three years. That memory was locked in her colon.

"She asked herself, 'Why do I believe I will die like my grandmothers?' The answer came in a visualization.

"As she grew older and closer to the time of her grandmothers' deaths, her stomach pains increased in intensity.

"Her subconscious memory had created an energy block in her stomach that contained all the memories of her fears.

"It wasn't until she heard about Medical Intuition that she was able to let go of her old fears and transform the energy block.

"The MIC had her visualize her colon in the color black. The color represented the unknown aspects of her stomach.

"She saw the energy block as a large, dark mass of ugliness. She often felt ugly and her MIC told her, 'Every time you feel like a failure, you put another layer on that energy block.'

"The woman was intelligent, but she allowed the most important people in her life to put her down. She hadn't realized that their criticism was creating more ugly energy in her colon.

"The MIC told her to visualize pink now, the color of self-love, in her colon. 'Instead of always trying to be perfect, let go and give yourself permission to err. Relax, play, and rest.'

"Her lifetime habits kept challenging her new way of thinking. To prevent falling into past cycles, her MIC had her create an audiotape to fill her body with positive suggestions. She realized her mother was a perfectionist, who had died from the inability to enjoy life to its fullest. She was duplicating that negative energy into her stomach as well.

"Why did this woman pull in all those negative energies? She did it because of her love and desire to heal. She was too young to understand why she couldn't heal, so she subconsciously punished herself instead.

"Part of her transformation was to envision her mother and grandmothers from her adult position. She then imagined a pipeline pulling their negative energy into a hot air balloon, sailing off into the atmosphere when it was full. Another pipeline poured white light into the empty parts of her stomach.

"She was to continue doing this exercise for 21 days to make it permanent.

"It took a series of MI sessions, but she was finally able to release the energy block in her body. Today this woman is free of guilt and colon pains."

You are amazed at hearing this story. Both your parents died early from painful diseases.

You ask yourself, "Do I feel guilty about not being able to help my parents get well?" The pains in your body intensify. Bingo!

※

Medical Intuition transforms energy blocks.

19

Knowing When to Say Yes

"WE GIVE AWAY OUR POWER when we don't trust our senses. Today you're going to learn how your bodies tell you when to say yes and when to say no," says our MIC.

"Imagination is the first step toward healing.

"Imagination takes you past your limitations.

"Meditation helps create a plan.

"Faith keeps you focused.

"Your actions make it happen.

"Close your eyes to shut off all external distractions. Breathe naturally in and out for a full minute as you imagine yourself in a lovely garden enjoying the flowers and birds. The day is beautiful and you're at peace.

"You're aware of the bees and the butterflies flying gently from flower to flower. The sun is shining soft, warm rays down on your body. All feels right in this garden.

> *"Everything that is really great and inspiring is created by the individual who can labor in freedom"*
> —ALBERT EINSTEIN, OUT OF MY LATER YEARS, 1950

"Suddenly you get a chill. The garden grows dark. You look around and see the most aggravating person you know entering your sanctuary.

"'How did he know where to find me?' you ask. You're getting upset and your body is beginning to ache. You don't want this person in your perfect garden.

"You want to push this person away. Instead I ask you to hold on to your thoughts to get more input.

"This negative feeling represents your 'no' response.

"Notice if your inhalation has become labored, or if you are having pains anywhere in your body. Do you feel insecure? Note as many negative symptoms as you can in the next two minutes.

"Exhale while visualizing this person leaving your garden.

"Wonderful, loving thoughts return as you see your best friend entering your sanctuary. He always makes you feel special. You extend your arms and hug one another. This is your friend. Focus on any physical or emotional changes occurring in your body and what thoughts enter your mind. Whenever you are in a quandary over making a decision, reflect back upon this person and connect with these feelings. This is your 'yes' response."

Write down your responses to the questionnaire on pages 81-82 as quickly as you can.

NO response:

1. Who was the tormentor?

_____

_____

2. Were the pains sharp or dull?

_____

_____

3. Where were the pains?

_____

_____

4. Was it difficult to breathe normally?

_____

_____

5. What thoughts came to mind?

_____

_____

6. What happened to your energy?

_____

_____

YES response:

1. Who was the friend?

_____

_____

2. What part of your body felt the greatest amount of joy?

_____

_____

3. What thoughts entered your mind?

_____

_____

4. What part of your body had the greatest amount of energy?

_____

_____

5. What colors did you notice in the garden?

_____

_____

6. Did you feel relaxed or energized?

_____

_____

Observe how easily your body shifted from negative to positive when you filled out the questionnaire.

Have you ever said, "This piece of cake will put five pounds on me"? Your body heard. Your body obeyed.

The "no" response is similar to the above statement. What you think will cause a energy reaction to your body. Obey your "no" response or take the consequences.

The "yes" response is generally harder to identify. Most people can't remember when their headache goes away, only when it hurts.

I remember one student's energy fading as he told the group his doctor had given him only six months to live. His "no" response was screaming.

Six months later, he was well and healthier. He had reclaimed his energy.

Test your "no/yes" response and know when to say "yes" and when to say "no."

✳

Medical Intuition means knowing
when to say yes and when to say no.

20

Don't Judge Yourself

THE STUDENTS ALL SPOKE AT ONCE. "Wait a minute! One at a time," said the MIC.

Student 1: "I had a busy week. Every time I got a no response, I listened without feeling defensive. Didn't have as many conflicts as I usually do."

Student 2: "I got a yes response to an idea I'd been thinking about. Talked it over with my boss and we are going to follow the idea further."

"A moment's insight is sometimes worth a life's experience."
—OLIVER WENDELL HOLMES, SR. IRIS, 1860

Student 3: "I don't like getting a no response when I want to eat chocolate."

Student 4: "I felt bad all week. Too many no responses."

MIC: "Please explain."

Student 4: "My boyfriend was out of town on business, he said, but my no response said differently. He doesn't always tell me the truth, but I didn't realize how often he lies."

MIC: "How did you feel your no response?"

Student 4: "My head felt like someone was tightening a steel band around it. It was hard to breathe and my legs were so weak. I couldn't stand."

MIC: "Who was the no response person in your garden?"

Student 4 looks at the floor. "My boyfriend."

You wanted to say something, but your throat felt constricted.

The MIC went on. "In the beginning you'll feel uncomfortable because you've been taught not to trust your senses. But soon you'll realize that you can make better decisions by knowing who to trust and when, which will give you more self trust."

You open your mouth to share, but nothing comes out. You feel alone and very tired.

"One of the problems of knowing when people lie is that they lie for a variety of reasons: social lies, business lies, lies to make themselves feel better, and lies about their personal relationships.

"Each time a person lies, his or her energy turns dark. The greater the lie, the darker the energy.

"Beginner Medical Intuition students tend to become very upset when they realize how many lies are being told by their favorite people.

"Try not to judge why they lie and try not to judge yourself too harshly when you lie.

"Can you remember a best friend asking for your opinion about a new opportunity? Did you tell the truth as you saw it? If you liked it, maybe. If you didn't, you probably told a little lie. Imagine selling an expensive item like your home or car. You might omit something to make the sale. A lie of omission.

"You might be lying to yourself when you say you'll go on a diet tomorrow. Today you want to enjoy that rich desert. Tomorrow comes and the lies continue.

"Don't stop loving yourself just because you didn't tell the whole truth and don't stop caring for others because of their lies."

※

Medical Intuition means not judging yourself or others.

21

You Can Be Wrong

"WHEN I WAS A TEENAGER, my father was an alcoholic and a smoker," began our MIC. "When his health became injured, I didn't understand why he couldn't stop his two vices. I became judgmental and refused to talk to him. I was sure he could stop if he wanted to bad enough.

"Freedom is not worth having if it does not connote freedom to err."
—MAHATMA GANDHI

"Later at his deathbed, he told me how hard he'd tried to stop smoking. He said, 'You don't know what an addiction is until you try to eliminate it from your life. I always thought I was a strong person, but that little cigarette beat me. Drinking was the only way I could be strong. I was wrong, but at the time, I thought I was right.' Then he died and I felt lower than the sidewalk.

"I became so guilt-ridden, I started eating mammoth amounts of sweets, mostly chocolates. I got a health problem and tried to cut out chocolates.

That's when I began to understand my dad's addictions. It's been twenty years and I still have to curb my sweet tooth.

"In every addiction lies a growth opportunity. In every disease lies the opportunity to understand ourselves better.

"My father wanted to be a great writer. He wasn't wealthy so he had to work at a job he didn't like to pay the bills. His responsibilities didn't allow much time for writing.

"He wanted success. He wanted fame. He did nothing to accomplish either desire. He smoked because he wasn't happy and drank for the same reason. He loved my mother, he just didn't love himself enough.

"All he wanted to do was write, but behind his writing desire was a fear that he was fooling himself. Did he have the talent? Perhaps he didn't. The irony was he had the gift of storytelling.

"What lesson did he need to learn?" the MIC asked the group.

Student 3: "He could have made the time to write if he stopped abusing himself."

Student 4: "I had a feeling that he had a good sense of humor about everyone except himself. He needed to have more fun in his life."

You raise your hand timidly. "I think your father loved his family so much, he didn't have anything left for himself."

The MIC's eyes grew moist. "You're all hitting the target. My father had low esteem, but he was good at his job. He loved my mother and my brothers and sisters. He just didn't love himself enough.

"He was always serious except when he was telling stories. Then he'd create the most marvelous characters and we'd all laugh at the trouble he'd get them into. He could have written stories about people who overcame self-rejection and helped others.

"Now I realize his growth opportunity was to love himself and because he didn't, he destroyed his liver and his lungs. A painful way to die."

Student 1: "Couldn't you help him?"

MIC: "I didn't know then what I know now. It's taken me many years to let go of my guilt. My growth opportunity was to let go of judging him and me.

"Many of you are suffering from guilt because you didn't handle a past relationship well. Those inner whiplashes cause energy blocks in your heart and cause a domino effect into the other vessels in your bodies.

"Judgment day isn't when you get to heaven, you do it every time you criticize yourself.

"Some of you may be reluctant to interfere in the lives of your loved ones because you're afraid of saying or doing the wrong thing.

"When you try to help and the wrong results occur, you blame yourself. It may or may not have been your fault. People make their own choices in spite of your best intentions.

"Give them permission to err and do the same for yourself. If you were perfect, you wouldn't be a mortal. You'd be a god and you wouldn't need any more growth opportunities."

✳

Medical Intuition is learning you can be wrong and still love yourself.

22

Loving Your Fears

You RETURN TO YOUR doctor. He takes more time examining you. He seems confused. He says, "Your tests came back with different readings. I had them rechecked before talking to you. Your disease has gone into a reverse cycle. I don't have any medical explanation. I don't want you to get your hopes too high. This could be a fluke. Let's repeat the tests in two months."

"He who has health, has hope, and he who has hope, has everything."

−ARABIAN PROVERB

Should you tell him what you've been doing? "Not yet," you tell yourself. "When the tests are repeated and your body is better, then maybe. Besides talking too soon might jinx your healing."

Will you tell the MC group? You don't know. You're excited about having this wonderful secret. Maybe they'll guess?

You walk further than you have in a long time and become exhausted. Your bubble bursts as you remember the doctor's warning, "Don't get your hopes too high."

You sleep a long time and wake trying to remember why you were so happy in the doctor's office. "So the tests showed some reverses. That doesn't mean anything. Before I got so sick, I had lots of reverses."

Your fury boils over. "Who am I kidding? I'll never lick this disease. The odds are against me. I don't want to live knowing I'll die in horrible pain. I'll end it all today."

You search the apartment for a tool to end your suffering. The knives aren't sharp enough. The ceiling isn't high enough to hang yourself. Don't own a gun. Can't jump out the window, you live on the first floor!

You look out the window and consider jumping in front of a truck or a train. But what if you're only injured, maybe lose a leg or arm?

You begin laughing at yourself. You can't stop and soon your laughter becomes hysterical. You fall back on your couch, tears streaming down your face.

"Have faith, my child," you hear.

"Who's talking?" you ask.

"You will be well," says the voice.

Your body relaxes and you fall into a deep sleep. You dream you are running away from something. You can't run fast enough. The fear monster is right behind you.

"Do not fear," says the voice.

You stop and turn toward the monster. "Who are you? Why are you in my life?"

"I'm your friend. I want to help you," says the monster, who doesn't look so scary now.

"How can you help me?"

"Love me. I won't hurt you."

"Love you. Why?"

"Just say it."

Reluctantly you say, "I love you."

The monster changes instantly into a beautiful lady wearing a flowing gown of pink. "You have transformed your fear into love, just like you will transform your disease. Trust."

You awake with a smile, anxious to share your experience with the group.

✳

Medical Intuition means loving your fears.

23

Loneliness Ends

You share your story with the group. Everyone begins hugging you and the others. You feel so loved, so wanted. Your body doesn't hurt anywhere. "That's a first," you say to yourself.

MIC: "People very seldom share their stories of healings. They'd much rather talk about their ailments than take the risk of sounding weird."

"Only eyes washed by tears can see clearly."
—LOUIS L. MANN

"You've taken a risk today," she points to you. "By talking aloud about your healing experience, you have cleaned the fuzz out of your body's computer. Incredible! What lesson have you learned?"

You stand up to answer. "I learned that I can control my thoughts, and help my body stop hurting. I don't know why I never knew that before. It seems so simple.

"Why didn't I tell my doctor what we've been doing here? What was I afraid of?"

"You were afraid of taking charge of your life. There is an awesome fear of taking control of your health," says the MIC.

"Medical people want to help you. They struggle to find the answers to what's wrong with your body. But they work in the dark because you don't know what to tell them. Imagine what they could accomplish if you aided them more.

"Dr. Jonas Salk wrote how he imagined himself as the polio germ. That's how he discovered the vaccine.

"You didn't want to be responsible for your healing. Your fear monster represented a lack of faith. Now you are thinking wellness, strength, and courage.

"You've come a long way toward understanding how you claimed your disease, but there is still more to learn.

"I'd like to talk about the voice you heard. There are many explanations, but here are two.

"The voice could have come from your higher consciousness — super-consciousness — the part of your mind that goes far beyond the physical dimension. Medical Intuition goes beyond what you know as possibility thinking.

"A second explanation might be that life goes on after our bodies cease to function. Perhaps it was your mother or your father at some higher level of mind consciousness, responding to your cry for help.

"Or perhaps a part of you woke up and wanted to live.

"The word disease is made up of two words, dis and ease. Dis . . . distant . . . separated . . . amiss. That's where you've been most of your life. Like the parts of a car lying on the ground waiting to be put back together, you've been waiting for a mechanic to make you whole and you didn't even know you were broke.

"Wherever the voice came from, you'll never longer feel alone again, because you're finally connected."

❋

Medical Intuition ends the loneliness.

24

Darkness Becomes Light

"The energies in your body flow around and around your body like the design of a paper clip, when you're healthy," began the MIC.

"Sickness can cause your energy flow to tear, build a dam, and or get sluggish. These disorders may cause aches, pains, and fear.

> *"When your fear decreases, your energy increases."*
> —RUTH BERGER, 1994

"Energy can easily be corrupted by being in an accident, or by fear. The wonder is that energy is never lost, just altered. Your thoughts can change the energy back to health.

"This exercise will help you 'see' your energy flow and locate where your energy is clogged up.

"Close your eyes and relax as much as you can. Slow your breathing down by following this formula:

"1. Inhale to the count of six;

"2. Hold your breath to the count of three;

"3. Exhale to the count of six;

"4. Do no breathing to the count of three;

"5. Repeat 1 — 4 six times.

"Imagine a pipeline of energy beginning at your left foot flowing up toward your head. The energy flows across your forehead down the right side of your body. When the energy reaches your right foot, it crosses over onto the left foot and goes around again.

"The color of your energy line represents how weak or strong it is. Relax and observe the color of the energy flow. Watch how the energy flow gets past the blockages or breaks in the line.

"Relax as you observe the energy flow. Keep watching. Don't judge what you see. Just be the observer. Do this for two minutes and then we'll talk."

Student 5 was first. "I saw the color red up until my right shoulder. Then the color changed to blue and then to dark purple. What does that mean?"

MIC: "Red may represent the color of your blood, or that you're excited about doing this process. The blue and the instant change to purple on your right shoulder indicates you think before using your intuitive energy to make decisions."

Student 5: "I do have a tendency to know things before other people do."

Student 3: "I saw indigo flowing through my entire body."

MIC: "Indigo is a healing color that moves at a very slow pace. Are you healing from an accident?"

Student 3 said, "Yes. I was hit by a car while crossing the street. I'm fine except for a sore foot, which seems to be healing slowly."

Student 7 spoke next. "I saw an electric bright blue line tracing my body very fast. The line got much brighter when it touched my left cheek. I thought it was because I'm smart. The color dimmed when it touched my right cheek."

MIC said, "Blue is the color of wisdom. The more electric the color, the deeper the level of knowledge.

"You said your energy line was racing in your head. Slow down. Your thoughts are moving too fast for your body."

Student 1 said excitedly, "I did it all. It was easy. My energy line had a fluorescent white glow except when it was passing through my hips. Then it turned dark and skinny. I've had a low back problem for years. Figured that was why it got dark there.

"I couldn't see the energy flowing across my head. I'm not sure why. I didn't judge what was happening because you said not to."

MIC said, "You told us you've been sick for a very long time, so you're probably more aware of your body. You need to change the way your energy flows so that your head and body are balanced.

"Close your eyes again and envision your energy flow again. Use your imagination and see the energy power line light up as it flows through your head.

"Pretend you're Walt Disney directing a movie. The bright power line is your hero and your head is the trapped heroine. Let your hero devise how he will save his special love."

Student 1 smiles. "I'm doing it. I can see the energy line lighting up my head as it passes through."

MIC smiles and says, "Enjoy the trip. Open your eyes when you're done."

Student 1 opens his eyes and says, "That was fun. I couldn't do it until you suggested Walt Disney. Then it was easy.

"I have a question. Something happened while I was viewing the power line flowing through my head. I saw a dark substance behind my eyes. I got scared. I remembered you saying, 'don't judge.' What was that dark blob?"

MIC responds. "It was an energy block in your 'inner seeing.' Somewhere in your past, you had a vision that came true. The experience was so scary, you shut down your ability to see intuitively.

"Children often shut off their inner seeing because they have a vision of someone dying. When the person dies similar to the vision, they feel responsible.

"You're no longer a child. You had a premonition, a warning about another person. You know you didn't cause the death of anyone.

"These experiences make you more aware. When your mind is open, you have more choices, which gives you more faith in your decision making abilities.

"The next step is to return to seeing the power line flowing through your head and watch it transform the dark blob behind your eyes into light."

✳

Medical Intuition transforms the darkness into light.

25

The Right Person

"I've had a whole month without pain. How is that possible?" you ask yourself. "Doctors told me I'd never get better, but I feel healthier and stronger than I've ever felt before.

"Am I setting myself up for a fall? Am I being hypnotized into thinking I'm better when I'm not?" You try to be depressed but you can't.

"Between two evils, choose neither; between two goods, choose both."

—TRYON EDWARDS

"Your body is a mystery to me. Nothing in the medical books talks about a reversal of your disease," said the doctor scratching his head. "You're getting better and I can't explain it. What are you doing differently?"

You're not sure if you should tell him. You decide to venture a little, "I've been meditating and visualizing my body in perfect health."

"Is that all?"

Fearful of being labeled a nut, you clamp your mouth shut.

The doctor says, "Okay. Let's keep an eye on your progress. Make an appointment for six months from now, unless you have an emergency. Then call me immediately."

You return to work whistling.

An employee enters your office to complain. "Boss. We've having trouble again with production. The machines just can't handle the overload."

Instead of reacting angrily as usual, you are intuitively aware of your employee's fear and the blockage in his self-trust. "What do I do now?" you ponder.

"Slow down," you remember MIC's training.

"Tell me what you think should be done," you ask your employee, who is stunned by your request.

"If I had enough money, I'd get one new machine and put all the overload on it."

"Do it," you say.

"Do it! All right," says the employee, running out the door before you can change your mind.

"Trusting is a new experience for me. We've needed a new machine for a year and I kept putting it off. Now I wonder why?"

A voice inside your head says, "You thought

you were dying. Now you know you're going to live, so you're making healthy choices."

You look around expecting to see the person who spoke. There is no one in your office. Instead of thinking, "I must be nuts," you laugh aloud and go through your messages.

The day passes quickly. A friend calls to invite you to dinner. You surprise yourself by accepting the invitation.

"I've been thinking a lot about you lately. How are you?" says your friend at dinner.

You decide to tell all. "I'm getting better. My doctor doesn't understand why, but I do! I want to tell you what I've been doing. Why my health has improved. I don't know why I decided to tell you my secret, but I'm going to trust you.

"Nine years ago I was diagnosed with a terrible disease. I went wild trying to find a doctor who could help me. No one changed the prognosis. Everyone confirmed my death would be very painful. I wanted to kill myself many times. I got divorced, just about ruined my business and almost lost my mind. I was so scared.

"I thought my future was bleak, until another friend called and invited me to a Medical Intuition seminar. I don't know why I went, but my life has been changing for the better ever since.

"I met people who had overcome terrible health problems. You know how skeptical I can be. I doubted everyone. But my pains got so bad, I'd have gone to a witch doctor to get better.

"These people study the mind in a way I'd never heard of before. They aren't weirdos. They just trust themselves more than most people I know. They use their sixth sense to know more.

"I used to have pain all the time. Now I haven't had any pain for over a month. That's just isn't possible with my disease. I'm happy most of the time now. You remember how angry I used to be at everyone?"

Your friend smiles and nods yes.

"I'm not angry any more. I'm not a lot of things. I'm not judgmental, or as skeptical. Instead of doubting what everyone says, I ask questions like a school-child. I find life fascinating. I awake looking forward to the day instead of dreading problems that might arise.

"I've always been curious. Now my curiosity is insatiable. I want to learn everything as fast as I can. I don't judge like I used to, I listen with all my senses, including my sixth sense."

You laugh at your friend's loud "WHAT?"

"Right. I never bought that nonsense before. Well I'm here to tell you that I not only accept intuition, I use it all the time and I'm about 60 percent accurate.

"I've learned that listening isn't just hearing the words. It's knowing why the person said them and what the hidden agenda was. You'd be amazed at the wealth of information you can get when you don't interrupt the speaker."

Your friend keeps smiling and waiting.

"At first I resented all their happy faces at the conference. Seemed to me they were letting themselves be taken down the river backwards. Don't judge, they said. I thought if you don't judge, you'll fall into every criminal's lap. Got to be careful, I used to think.

"They taught me how to know when to say yes or no. Not through doubt, but through my body's energy scanner. You know, our bodies are pretty terrific."

"Yes I know," says your friend.

Three hours later, you stop talking.

Your friend says, "I joined a Medical Intuition study group some twenty years ago when I wanted to end my life. I wasn't sick physically, just dying emotionally.

"You don't remember my best friend dying of leukemia. I felt so bad, so helpless, I wanted to end it all.

"Just like you, someone called me and I answered.

"There are no coincidences, just opportunities. I think you felt comfortable sharing with me because we're walking the same path. I'm glad your shared your story with me."

A woman at the next table turned to us with tears in her eyes, "I didn't mean to listen, but God must have put me next to your table. My doctor just told me I have a only few months to live. Can I join your group?"

"Yes," we both said in unison.

✳

Medical Intuition connects you with the right person at the right time.

26

Use Your Fears as Tools

THE WOMAN SPOKE SO quietly, most of the group couldn't hear. "Speak up," said Student 1.

The woman lifted her head and spoke louder. "Everyone I ever loved has died. My parents were killed in a plane crash when I was 5. My twin sister was killed by a burglar two years ago and my husband died last year from cancer.

"I'm afraid of dying alone, with no one caring if I live or die," she sobbed.

"Fear is an insidious disease," said MIC, "that isolates you and limits you. Fear decreases your creativity flow and increases health problems.

"Using the word 'fear' as a catalyst toward creative solutions, each of you who wants to help transform this woman's fears will pretend to be someone fictitious or real, living or dead.

> *"At every step, one has to wrestle for truth; one has to surrender to it almost everything to which the heart, to which our love, our trust in life clings otherwise."*
> —FRIEDRICH W. NIETZSCHE

"When you wish to talk, sit in the empty chair directly opposite her."

Your friend has done this technique before and immediately sits in the empty chair. "I am going to pretend to be David from the Bible who is going to slay your fear giant.

"I know the best way to diminish your fear giant is to love him. The more you fear him, the larger he becomes. He gains power through your fears. Give him love and you will not be fearful any longer."

Student 1 was next to sit in the chair. "I'm pretending to be Helen Keller. I was so angry at everyone. No one understood my needs. I fought, I spit, I was frightened. I couldn't hear. I couldn't see and I hated being me.

"My tutor helped me to use those parts of me that worked. Through patience and love she taught me to accept who I was and what I could do.

"Now I am your tutor. Stop fighting yourself. Use the parts of you that work."

Student 8 said, "I am going to pretend to be your dead mother. I didn't plan to leave you so early. I wanted to give you pretty dresses, dance lessons, take you to concerts and mostly, hold you and love you.

"Since I entered this other place you call heaven, I've been able to watch you pursue life with amazing strength and intelligence.

"If I'd lived, you might not have become so strong. I would have overprotected you and your sister.

"I love you. You have a choice, my daughter, so I've been told by the angels. You can stop living right now, this moment, or you can use whatever time you have to help others. The choice is yours."

Student 5: "I'm pretending to be Eleanor Roosevelt who used to be afraid because she wanted to be just like the people she admired. The more she tried to emulate them, the more she was afraid to be herself. You see she didn't like herself very much.

"The first time she tried to speak publicly, she fainted. Later she learned that her fears were nothing compared to the people who needed to hear her words on hope.

"She stopped being afraid to speak when she focused on their needs, not hers. People who do not have hope, live and die in fear."

Student 2 said, "Walt Disney is my name. Every new idea I had was objected to by the bankers. They said, it couldn't be done . . . it would cost too much . . . no one would come.

"When I followed my dreams, I had no fears. It was only when I doubted me, that I lost faith."

Student 3 was next. "I'm pretending to be the richest man in the world in my heart and in my bank. I can do anything . . . buy anything . . . be anything.

"Fear is for people who don't have prosperity. Fear is for people who don't think success. I give you the gift of prosperity thinking. You can everything you want."

The woman challenged the student, "You can't buy my husband's life back."

Student 3: "Perhaps not. But I can search the world to find another mate for you, perhaps a richer one."

The woman laughed.

Student 4: "I'm pretending to be Lassie, the TV wonder dog. I can't speak like a human, but I'm resourceful and courageous. Nothing daunts me. I'm a hero. I've come here to save you.

"Hold on to my collar and we'll swim out of the river of negative emotions. Once we get on positive soil, my trainer will teach you how to survive. Don't be afraid. He's very nice."

Student 5 says, "I'm pretending to be Carl Jung, the noted Swiss psychologist.

"When I studied with Sigmund Freud, I thought he was the teacher and I, the student. He was brilliant. It took me years to discover my own talent for understanding symbols and dreams.

"I had to become aware of a higher level of the mind that I called universal consciousness, which holds the answers to all of life's questions.

"You are never alone when you tap into universal consciousness. You are never alone when you have a dream."

When the others are done, you sit in the empty chair and begin, "I am not going to pretend to be someone else. I've been doing that all my life. I'm going to be the real me.

"I've been angry most of my life. I thought anger gave me power. I was wrong. Anger is just another level of fear.

"When my first child was born, I was angry because she had a birth defect. My anger was a blanket for my fear of not understanding the reason for her problem and what to do about it.

"The doctor said the chances of having another child with birth defects were 400 to 1. My second child was born with multiple birth defects. I was furious at the inconsistencies of the doctor.

"I thought doctors knew everything. I had made my doctor a God. When my 'human God' made a mistake, my anger multiplied. I know now that I was frightened of losing my faith in the medical profession.

"The specialists told us not to have any more children. They said the odds were too high that a third child would be born mentally retarded.

"When the third child was born normal, I was relieved, but furious that the doctors had been wrong again. How could I trust them ever again?

"Through the years, I lost more trust in doctors when my mother and my best friend died of cancer. Why couldn't their pain be eliminated? Why did they have to die? I asked the doctors.

"I didn't want to trust any doctor, but I had to sometimes. When I got injured in an automobile accident, I went to a bone specialist. He couldn't help me. My pains increased and so did my anger. I was afraid of being in pain for the rest of my life because no one would be able to help me.

"Sixty years of anger. Sixty years of fears multiplying before I realized how to use my fears to heal my body. Fear is energy. Fear helps us to be aware.

"I've read everything I can about my disease. I don't put my doctor on a pedestal any more. I talk to my doctor like I would a *business partner*. I want to know everything I can about my disease so I, not others, can make decisions about my healing process.

"My assumption about doctors being Gods has been laid to rest. We work together, not separately. That gives me power and makes me less angry.

"Don't be afraid of your fears. Use your fears as a tool to gain back your power."

✳

Medical Intuition helps you use your fears as tools.

27

Creating Love and Order

"MIND EXPANSION CAN BE similar to a first solo driving experience; scary, wonderful, exciting, horrible," said the MIC.

"I had to drive to the downtown section of Chicago for my child's medical checkup. I should have been afraid, but I was too excited about the opportunity of driving my car without a copilot.

"The art of progress is to preserve order amid change, and to preserve change amid order. Life refuses to be embalmed alive."

—ALFRED NORTH WHITEHEAD

"Downtown Chicago is like suddenly being thrust into a madhouse. Taxi cab drivers shooting in and out, trying to be the first to pick up a fare—huge buses entering a lane without warning—and pedestrians scurrying across the streets without concern for life or limb.

"The first time a cab driver shot in front of me, I was no longer excited about driving. In fact, I wanted to leave the car right where it was, in the middle of the traffic, and take the bus home.

"If the drivers weren't enough to unnerve me, trying to park my car was a bigger nightmare.

"My husband had suggested that I park my car in the underground parking lot. The entrance was facing the wrong way, so I had to drive another six blocks in all that traffic before I found a policeman to ask what to do.

"He said, 'Drive a few blocks north and you'll see a circular driveway. You can turn your car around and backtrack.'

"Frantically I drove to the circular driveway only to discover a car was broken down in it. There wasn't enough room for me to get past him.

"Another policeman said, 'Just drive across the bridge at the right time, make a U-turn in front of the oncoming traffic. Just be quick.'

"I asked the policeman to drive my car for me, but he declined. 'You can do it,' he said. I didn't think so.

"Feeling like a kamikaze pilot on his last mission, I made the U-turn with the traffic coming toward me. Thank God! All I wanted to do was park the car and call my husband to come and get us.

"As I got closer to the underground parking entrance, I saw a barrier in front with a big sign that read 'full.' I panicked. Where was I going to park now?

"I drove an extra six blocks and found a parking space in the garage next door to my doctor's office.

"The final blow was the doctor's nurse saying my appointment wasn't for another week. After I burst out crying from all the tension, she said she could fit me in.

"When I told people about my experience, they laughed and were amazed that I'd gone downtown for my first day of driving.

"Mind expansion is just like my first day of driving. You don't know what will happen next. People will help you, but in the final test, you have to drive alone.

"Confusion and frustration will create impatience, which will exacerbate the feelings of disorder in your life. Realize you are in the midst of change. Don't be frustrated because you can't see the future yet.

"As a child, you learned to walk and talk by observing and imitating others. You have no guidelines now, no calendars to tell you how long it will take you to balance your inner world with your outer world.

"You'll see people you love doing things and making decisions that don't make sense to you. They're not aware of what you're aware of.

"Be patient with them. Don't try to convert them to your new way of believing, and be patient with yourself.

"Your old way of handling situations was to believe that authority figures knew more about your body than you did. This changes as you take charge of your life. You'll be making decisions like who will be your friend . . . what will you do with the rest of your life . . . how will you begin to put your life in order?

"Sickness is a disorder in the mind and body. Beginning your day with disorder disrupts your body's energy and confusion sets in. Fear is disorder, love is order.

"This exercise will help you create a daily discipline to sustain yourself through the coming changes.

"Select a place and a time of the day where you can spend ten minutes in a peaceful meditation without interruption.

"1. Mentally affirm, 'I am at peace,' while inhaling to the count of six.

"2. Hold your breath for a count of three.

"3. Visualize negative energy flowing out of your body as you exhale to the count of six.

"4. Do nothing for the count of three.

"5. Repeat the four steps six times.

"6. Meditate on what you need to understand about the day.

"7. Meditate on what you are resisting.

"8. Keep a journal of your meditations and responses.

"Whenever you become fearful, repeat the exercise and add an extra ten minutes for relaxation."

✳

Medical Intuition creates love and order in your life.

28

Learning About Your Illness

"Most people enter hospitals because they're in pain. Imagine people going to hospitals to prevent them from getting sick.

"You feel fine now. Why not take some tests that will put your mind at ease and tell you what you need to know for future protection," suggests MIC.

"There is no instinct like that of the heart."

—LORD BYRON

"That makes sense," you think. "I'll call my doctor and check it out."

You explain to the doctor what you'd like to do.

He says, "Great. I'll set it up."

"I have one request. No invasive testing unless I agree there's a good reason."

"No problem. That's a reasonable request."

There are three other patients in your hospital room. Patient 1 is having therapy and tests for back pain. Patient 2 is nervous about having gallbladder surgery in the morning. Patient 3 sleeps most of the time because of pain. You're the only healthy person in the room.

Patient 1's doctor holds court in our little hospital room. His two assistants run to keep up with him. The doctor shrugs off the patient's questions by saying, "Don't worry. Just take it easy and rest." He pats the patient's shoulder and leaves the room. Total visit was less than three minutes.

You hear the patient whisper, "I wish I knew what was wrong with me."

"Why are you here?" you ask.

"I'd been having a lot of pain in my lower back, especially at work. Last week I tried to get up from my desk and couldn't. The paramedics brought me to this hospital. Every day for the past week I've taken tests, but no one will tell me anything and my back still hurts."

You fall asleep wondering why this patient can't get any answers and have the following dream:

The patient has to bike a hundred miles over pitted roads. Spouse is driving a car with six passengers. There are hundreds of people walking on the road, migrating from their village. There's hardly any space for the patient to ride the bike.

The spouse says, "There's enough room for you and your bike in the car. You don't have to do it the hard way." End of dream.

You share your dream with the patient who asks, "What am I doing the hard way? I don't have a clue."

"Say the word 'hard' over and over. See if it brings up anything."

Patient: "I'll try anything. Hard, hard work, hard boss, hard job, hard back, no flexibility, stubborn, hardheaded."

You: "When did your back problem begin?"

Patient looks away: "About five years ago I lost the only person who ever meant anything to me. Ever since, life has been hard."

A few minutes of silence pass before you ask: "What does a pitted road mean to you?"

Patient: "A pitted road is a neglected road."

You: "Have you been neglecting yourself?"

Patient blushes: "Yeah! I don't like to cook just for me. I hate eating by myself. Most of the time I eat junk food."

You laugh: "Sounds hard on your stomach! What does a bicycle represent to you?"

Patient: "Bicycle! I haven't ridden one in years. Used to love to ride a bike."

You: "Do you get any exercise?"

Patient: "Not much. Always going to join a health club, but when my back hurts, I put it off."

You: "I don't know much about you, but I think you ought to read up on back problems and learn as much as you can about your medical choices. Seems to me you're going about things the hard way, the slow way. Why don't you write out your questions so when the doctor comes, you won't get flustered?"

Patient doesn't say anything. You leave to take a test.

The patient asks the nurse for literature on back problems. When you return, the patient has pamphlets sprawled on the bed and is writing a list of questions.

When the doctor visits again, the patient shows him the list and they discuss the questions.

The next day the patient asks if you've had another dream.

"Yes," you say. "I dreamt about you again. The road had been repaired and you were riding a motorcycle. You were radiant with good health."

Patient: "I had a dream too. In the dream my body was saying to trust me more. From now on, I'm going to read and ask more questions and put more time into finding the right doctor. I'm going to search for the right doctor, the way companies do for employees. Thanks for all your insights."

✳

Medical Intuition means learning more about your illness.

29

Finding the Right Healer

Patient 2's doctor came in and explained the surgical procedure he'd be doing in the morning. The patient smiled and agreed with everything the doctor said.

The patient turned and tossed all night. Morning came and the nurses took the patient to surgery.

Happiness depends upon ourselves."
—ARISTOTLE

Still filled with the aftereffects of anesthesia, the patient said, "Thank God it's over," and quickly fell back to sleep.

You overhear a patient in the next room talking to her doctor. "The surgeon's hands were shaking and he couldn't remember my name. I'm afraid of him operating on me."

Doctor says, "Now, now. Don't you trust me? I wouldn't worry about the surgeon. He's done hundreds of these surgeries and never lost a patient yet."

"Can't you suggest anyone else?" she asks.

"You're getting overwrought. Trust me," the doctors pats her shoulder and walks away.

The patient begins to cry.

You walk into her room and ask, "What's the matter?"

"I'm terrified. Yesterday, the surgeon my doctor recommended came to see me. He kept calling me by the wrong name. I corrected him three times and he still didn't know who I was, and his hands were shaking, too!

"My doctor thinks I'm being silly. Tomorrow is the operation. I don't know what to do."

"What do you want to do?" you ask.

"Run like hell."

"It sounds like you should trust your instincts."

"What if I'm wrong? What if my doctor is right and I'm being silly. I might make him angry."

"What if he's wrong?"

"I don't know what to do," the woman says as she buries her head in the pillow and cries.

A few hours later, the woman gets a temperature. The operation is postponed temporarily. The woman is discharged.

Later your MIC visits you in the hospital and explains what happened to the woman.

"The woman lost her power when she became afraid of making the wrong decision. She was lucky.

Her body took over and created a temperature to avoid the surgery.

"Every cell in her body was screaming no. She heard the noise in her mind, but wasn't strong enough to follow through, so her cells took over.

"Cells are energy guards at work in the body at all times. They were trying to tell her, 'We need you to pay attention to what's happening. The more you ignore us, the more pain your body will have. We've got to get you to listen.'

"Surgery helps reduce the pain, but it doesn't answer why the problem got there in the first place. More study is needed by this woman to get to the root of why and when the problem actually began."

※

Medical Intuition means finding the right healer.

CHAPTER 30

The Root of Your Disease

Patient 3 is awakened by the doctor. "How are you?"

No response.

The doctor looks at the untouched tray of food. "The nurses say you aren't eating. You've got to eat."

Patient mumbles. Doctor leaves.

The scene is repeated at every meal.

Nurse wakes the patient. "You've haven't eaten anything. You'll never get well if you don't eat something."

Patient doesn't respond. Nurse leaves.

"Living is a disease from which sleep gives us relief eight hours a day."

—SEBASTIEN RICH
NICOLAS CHAMFORT

For three days, you observe nurses and doctors talking to the sleeping patient, who always mumbles and never takes a sip of water or eats a bite of food.

On the third day, after visiting hours, the patient's spouse walks in yelling, "You leave me to do everything while you just lie there. You're selfish!

All you do is sleep." The spouse shook the bed, saw no response, and said upon leaving, "I wish you were dead."

The back pain patient said aloud, "If I was married to that person, I wouldn't want to wake up either."

Instantly the sleeper's eyes open and look directly at the other patient. "I'm hungry," said the sleeper.

The nurses were only too happy to bring a tray of food. The sleeper ate everything and dozed off again.

"What made the sleeper wake up? Was it the words of sympathy uttered by the other patient? Was it the spouse's frustration? What is wrong with this person?" Your curiosity is aroused.

During the night, while the other patients sleep, you and the sleeper talk.

"Why are you here?" you ask.

"It's the only place I can get some rest."

"Do you have a medical problem?"

"Yes. I have lots of them: diabetes, migraines, seizures. I just want to die most of the time. I'm too big a coward, or I'd have committed suicide by now."

You say calmly, "We all die a little every night. Death is no stranger to you or me. Maybe you just want to change a part of your life and don't know how, so you think about killing all of you, the good parts, too."

"There are no good parts."

Struggling for ways to help this patient, you ask, "What did you want to be when you were growing up?"

Patient sneers, "I used to dream I'd be a famous writer someday. Big dream. Big letdown.

"My father didn't think I'd ever amount to anything. He used to tell everyone how stupid I was.

"My mother was a wimp. She'd never stood up for herself or her children. Just let our drunken father beat the tar out of us all.

"I left home at 16 determined to show him. The only thing I've done is become more like my mother, a wimp. I'm letting the world beat me down. You heard my spouse, who is like my cruel father and never saw my pain either."

You say, "So you set out to prove your father right?"

"Of course not. I did everything I could, but nothing worked. It's not easy out there in the real world. No one ever helped me. Now it's too late. I'm going to die."

"How do you know you're going to die?"

"You mean like did the doctors tell me. Hell no! All they do is have me take more tests because they don't know what to do."

Where had you heard that before?

"I'm going to die because I have no luck. Whatever is wrong with me won't have a solution.

And that's okay with me. Got nothing to live for anyway."

"I used to feel the same way. The doctors told me I had a disease that would kill me. They said I'd die in excruciating pain. They were wrong.

"At first I was like you, fed up and wanting to die. My life was a mess. I got divorced and wallowed in self pity.

"My disease advanced and so did my pains. I couldn't sleep or get any relief. All I wanted was to get out of this world as soon as possible. I spent hours thinking of all the ways I could kill myself. Don't know what kept me from doing it.

"One day a friend called and invited me to a Medical Intuition seminar. I looked just as puzzled then as you do now. I asked what it was, but my friend just said, 'You'll see.'

"I went in a skeptic and emerged wondering if I could change my disease into an opportunity to learn more about me.

"The speakers talked about diseases being more than a physical illness. They said, 'Most diseases begin in early childhood when the child makes an incorrect assumption about someone or something, and locks in negative energy. More traumas, more negative energy. The disease explodes when the body can't hold any more negative energy.'

"The beauty of it all is there are ways to transform the negative energies. The more you know about the way you handle life's problems, the better able you are at finding the root cause of your problem.

"Anger was a major problem in causing my disease. I learned that my anger manifested when I was unable to understand a person or a situation. My anger covered up my fear of not being able to resolve the problem.

"Now I use my anger as a tool. I ask myself questions such as: who, what am I angry about? Or, what is it I am resisting? Or, what's between God and me?"

The patient interrupts. "What do you mean, what's between God and me?"

"I learned this technique in Medical Intuition. Let me give you an example first.

"When I got my disease, I was angry at God. That anger separated me from God. The anger grew in me until I got so much pain that I began to pray for help.

"I imagined a white light streaming down from heaven in front of me. I envisioned me putting my anger in a black box. I put the box behind me.

"The light represented God. I asked the light, 'What was I resisting?' I heard the answer loud and clear in my mind, 'You are resisting change. Let go of the past. Let go of your anger. Trust yourself more and doubt less.'

"Crazy as it may sound, I did what the voice said and found peace. I heard the voice often, but didn't always listen. It took me awhile to surrender my stubbornness. I thought being angry kept me from trusting the wrong people, making the wrong decisions. Wrong!

"Anger kept me from seeing more options. Just like you, I closed my mind off from others."

Tears were streaming down the patient's eyes. "I never thought I was angry until now. Do you think I could join your group?"

You nod yes.

＊

*Medical Intuition means discovering
the root of your disease.*

31

Making Choices

You had two days of tests before you said no to your doctor. All tests showed you were in ideal health. There was no reason given for an invasive test. The doctor agreed it wasn't necessary. You declined the test.

"The difficulty in life is the choice."

—GEORGE MOORE

Later that evening, the nurse came to prepare you for the invasive test scheduled for the morning.

You advised her you had canceled the test.

She said the doctor hadn't.

The hospital doctor came to see you. He was patient, but firm.

You say, no invasive test!

Your phone rings. It's your doctor trying to change your mind. He didn't.

In the morning, another nurse tries to prepare you for the test. You explain. She doesn't care. She storms out of the room.

The gallbladder patient yells, "How dare you not do what the doctor tells you to do? Who do you think you are? God?"

You are shocked at the sudden verbal outburst from this patient. Why the anger? Your thoughts are interrupted again.

"You question everything. Don't you know doctors are busy people. Why can't you just go along with the program?"

"What is this person afraid of," you wonder? Intuitively you are aware the patient's energy flow is racing faster and faster. The thought enters your mind, "This patient has made doctors into gods! I'm challenging this person's beliefs. How do I handle the situation?"

You leave the room to walk in the hall. You focus on a ray of light pouring through the window at the end of the corridor. Soon your body fills with the light and you ask God, "What do I need to understand about what just happened?"

You hear a voice in your head saying, "Choices! You choose to honor your beliefs. You trusted yourself. You asked questions and made a decision based on the answers. You accepted the responsibility for your choice.

"Your roommate didn't want to accept any responsibility for the gallbladder problem. It was easier to have the doctor, an authority figure, decide what was best. The patient was content with that choice until you disagreed with the doctor.

"You showed courage in spite of the nurses' and doctors' pressure to change your mind. You had your belief and you followed through.

"This patient finds you confusing and is angry because you stand firm on your beliefs. Go back to your room and act as if nothing has happened."

You return to an apology from the gallbladder patient. "I'm sorry. I didn't mean to take my frustrations out on you. All my life I've been wanting to do what you did today. I hated you for showing me what a coward I've been.

"I heard you talking last night about your Medical Intuition study group. Got room for another person?"

You nod yes.

*

Medical Intuition means making choices.

32

Knowing Your Rights

MIC: "I remember saying to a good friend, 'Call the doctor. The medicine you're taking isn't agreeing with you.'

"She said, 'I don't want to bother the doctor. I'm going to see him next week. I'll ask him then.'

"I said, 'Doctors practice medicine. They are not Gods. They give you the medicine they think will do the best job. You may have a negative reaction to the drug. Unless you tell them, they won't know.'"

"To be conscious that you are ignorant is a great step to knowledge."
—BENJAMIN DISRAELI, SYBIL (1845), 5

You remember a friend telling you about her experience with doctors. She said, "My first child was born with a cleft palate. The doctor said the chances of it happening to my second child were 400,000 to 1. My second child was born with multiple birth defects.

"The doctors said not to have any more children because the odds of having a mentally retarded child were very high.

"It was a shock when I got pregnant against all odds. My third child was the only one born normal."

MIC continues, "The more you know about your patient rights, the more you will discover how to work with your doctor. A true healing is one in which an illness or disease is totally eradicated from the body.

"Doctors and patients must partner if a total cure is to be accomplished. The more input you can give your doctor, the more he or she can assist you in getting well—both accepting responsibility for all healing decisions."

✳

Medical Intuition means knowing your rights.

The Medical Intuition Bill of Rights

You have the right to:

- Overcome all odds;

- Be in perfect health;

- Pursue your health in any way you wish;

- Ask as many questions as you require to understand;

- Deny any medical treatment;

- Ask for second opinions;

- Try alternative treatment;

- Be stupid about the medical field;

- Decide which treatment is best.

✳

33

Healing the Mind

You've been asked to speak at a Medical Intuition conference about how you overcame your disease.

You begin by saying, "I was lucky. It took me ten years to overcome a horrible disease that has killed thousands of people. My sickness helped me not only to get well, but to find a better way to live.

"I thought getting rid of my disease would be all I've ever wanted or needed. I didn't realize how much healing I really required.

"I wanted a miracle. I wanted the doctors to find a technique that would rid my body of the disease. When they couldn't give me that miracle, I got angry.

"I hated them. I hated being sick. I hated my body. My real sickness was hate.

> *"Much of your pain is self-chosen. It is the bitter potion by which the physician within you heals your sick self."*
> —KAHLIL GIBRAN, "ON PAIN," THE PROPHET (1923)

"My hate cost me my marriage, and almost my life.

"Illness entered my body because I was empty inside. I had to learn how to fill that emptiness with healthy, loving thoughts, or die.

"It wasn't until I found hope that I was able to change the sickness within me.

"Hope helped me understand how destructive my fears were. I learned the more I feared, the more I destroyed me.

"I worried my family couldn't survive without me. I feared for my business, for my friends, for the world. I didn't know I had to let go of my fears. I didn't realize how much fear influenced all my decisions.

"The first time I heard a disease was a 'growth opportunity,' I got furious. I thought the speaker was nuts. I've since changed my mind. I've grown more wise. I've learned to love.

"A disease is an opportunity to be reborn.

"The last ten years have been the worse and the best years of my life. I had to change how I breathed, ate, slept, exercised, thought, lived, and it was rough.

"I had to give up my only addiction, sugar. In the old days, my lunches usually consisted of a chocolate candy bar and a milkshake. I never gained weight, so sugar wasn't a problem, I thought.

"My next hurdle was to change the way I'd been breathing all my life. I spent a lot of time concentrating on breathing correctly.

"I woke at 4:00 A.M. every day to do 30 minutes of yoga because it was my only free time.

"My priorities were work first, family second, and my health, when and if I had time.

"I had to change and make health my top priority. That wasn't easy.

"Another change occurred when I realized my working out other people's problems just made them weaker and more dependent on me.

"Now I help those people brainstorm to come up with their own solutions.

"I learned healing is sharing an idea and offering hope. Worry just burned up my body.

"Now I start each day with a prayer and meditation.

"If I have a question about something or someone, I imagine people like Ghandi, or Joan of Arc, or Moses, or Jesus offering me sage advice. It gives me a different perspective on the situation. Visualizing power and positive people expands my energy field.

"I keep a journal now and write everything down. Later I study it.

"I made all my life changes because I didn't feel I had a choice. I could get well or get sicker and die.

"The attacks from the disease kept me focused. The changes made me feel powerful.

"I learned to direct my sensitivity.

"If I get a phone call about someone suffering, I don't take on the pain like I used to. I just imagine a light pouring down over my body and visualize the person in pain, feeling the light. Then I ask God to take over.

"I am committed to always keeping my light bright and my fears small. My body deserves to be healthy and so does yours."

✳

Medical Intuition heals the mind.

Please
Share

Please share this book with meeting planners, clients, patients, friends, and loved ones, so we can work together to help people become active participants to take control of their healing process.

"A desire of knowledge is the natural feeling of mankind, and every human being, whose mind is not debauched, will be willing to give all that he has to get knowledge."
—Samuel Johnson, 1763

Illness doesn't get cured by getting rid of the pain. Illness comes because there is an emptiness somewhere in the person's life. Emptiness must be filled with healthy thoughts or the person will get sick again.

Everyone needs hope. Everyone needs faith. People want miracles. People resist change. When the body's health is restored, the mind must also be healed. The mind created the illness, therefore the mind must heal the illness.

Change is part of the healing.

Helping others eases you into change.

Helping others enables you to "see" multiple options.

Helping others increases your creativity.

❋

When everyone knows how to use Medical Intuition we will see the end of all diseases.

About the Author

Ruth Berger, intuitive training consultant, TV and radio personality, author and speaker, is an internationally recognized authority in the field of intuition. She travels throughout the United States and Canada doing ESP demonstrations, lectures and workshops.

Her first book, *The Secret is in the Rainbow: Aura Interrelationships*, is published by Weiser and has been translated into Spanish and Portuguese. Ruth lives in Illinois with her family.

Ruth is available for speaking engagements and consultations. You can contact her directly by calling (708) 676-4900.